A General Introduction to the Series

THIS series has been undertaken in the conviction that there can be no subject of study more important than history. Great as have been the conquests of natural science in our time—such that many think of ours as a scientific age *par excellence*—it is even more urgent and necessary that advances should be made in the social sciences, if we are to gain control of the forces of nature loosed upon us. The bed out of which all the social sciences spring is history; there they find, in greater or lesser degree, subject-matter and material, verification or contradiction.

There is no end to what we can learn from history, if only we would, for it is coterminous with life. Its special field is the life of man in society, and at every point we can learn vicariously from the experience of others before us in history.

To take one point only—the understanding of politics: how can we hope to understand the world of affairs around us if we do not know how it came to be what it is? How to understand Germany, or Soviet Russia, or the United States—or ourselves, without knowing something of their history?

There is no subject that is more useful, or indeed indispensable.

Some evidence of the growing awareness of this may be seen in the immense increase in the interest of the

reading public in history, and the much larger place
the subject has come to take in education in our time.

This series has been planned to meet the needs and
demands of a very wide public and of education—they
are indeed the same. I am convinced that the most
congenial, as well as the most concrete and practical,
approach to history is the biographical, through the
lives of the great men whose careers in turn have been
so moulded and formed by events.

The key idea of this series, and what distinguishes
it from any other that has appeared, is the intention
by way of a biography of a great man to open up a
significant historical theme; for example, Cromwell
and the Puritan Revolution, or Lenin and the Russian
Revolution.

My hope is, in the end, as the series fills out and
completes itself, by a sufficient number of biographies
to cover whole periods and subjects in that way. To
give you the history of the United States, for example,
or the British Empire or France, *via* a number of
biographies of their leading historical figures.

That should be something new, as well as con-
venient and practical, in education.

I need hardly say that I am a strong believer in
people with good academic standards writing once
more for the general reading public, and of the public
being given the best that the universities can provide.
From this point of view this series is intended to bring
the university into the homes of the people.

A. L. ROWSE.

ALL SOULS COLLEGE
OXFORD.

ERASMUS

and the

Northern Renaissance

by
MARGARET MANN PHILLIPS

THE ENGLISH UNIVERSITIES PRESS LTD
ST PAUL'S HOUSE   WARWICK LANE
LONDON EC4

First Printed	1949
Second Impression	1959
Third Impression	1961
Fourth Impression	1964
Fifth Impression	1967

SBN 340 05845 5

PRINTED AND BOUND IN ENGLAND
FOR THE ENGLISH UNIVERSITIES PRESS LTD
BY HAZELL WATSON AND VINEY LTD, AYLESBURY

Contents

With gratitude

to

M. AUGUSTIN RENAUDET
Professeur au Collège de France

Foreword

THIS book is primarily intended for the use of beginners in Renaissance studies. It does not claim to make new discoveries in a field where so many distinguished scholars have laboured, or rather disported themselves in company with one of the most attractive personalities known to history. But any portrait of Erasmus can fitly bear the title chosen by one biographer:[1] "a study in restatement"; and any such study which interprets for the English reader some of the recent works of foreign scholarship may have its uses. The whole field of Erasmian studies has been illuminated by M. Augustin Renaudet's brilliant and sympathetic analysis[2] of Erasmus's years at Bâle, with their plans, uncertainties, controversies and problems, and especially of the writings that were the fruit of those years. The possession of the whole wonderful series of Erasmus's Letters,[3] in an impeccable and satisfying form, is England's own gift to scholarship, and simplifies the whole problem. But it is possible that owing to their very significance Erasmus has been seen too much through his letters, which reveal his delightfully human foibles as well as his deeper side, and not enough through the voluminous works which he left as his legacy to his friends. An analysis

[1] The Rev. Elliott Binns, *Erasmus the Reformer: a study in restatement*, Cambridge, 1921–2.

[2] A. Renaudet, *Etudes Erasmiennes*, Paris, 1939.

[3] P. S. & H. M. Allen, *Erasmi Epistolae*, Oxford, 1906–47.

such as M. Renaudet's is the surest way to correct this. And if this little book succeeds in putting at the disposal of English readers who have no Latin, both the findings of recent research and a summary of the content of some of Erasmus's most important writings, it will have served its purpose.

Portrait

"IF anyone had taken me to see Erasmus in old days, I should have expected nothing to fall from his lips but adages and maxims, even in speaking to his servant and the hostess of his inn." So said Montaigne; Erasmus was pictured in his mind as the man of proverbs, the collector of the *Adagia*, that enormous bedside book for the would-be classical scholar. Montaigne himself had richly profited from the short cuts to learning it provided. In thinking of Erasmus thus, as a populariser of the classics, he was taking one of the simplest and most widespread causes for Erasmus's fame; but how many other notions have been held as to Erasmus's significance in history! Alternately adopted and anathematised by both Protestant and Catholic, in his own age and in later ages—seen by the eighteenth century as a rationalist and precursor of enlightened agnosticism, by the nineteenth as an apostle of liberty and peace, by the twentieth as a symbol of international understanding—his personality has been put to varied uses and figured as the supporter of many a cause. Through it all he preserves the same enigmatic half-smile, and remains one of the most vividly alive of the strongly marked individualists of a brilliant age.

The most constant and least controversial way to look at Erasmus is as the greatest representative of the Renaissance in Northern Europe. However current

views on him have varied, emphasising now one facet
and now the other of a complicated mind, everyone
has always agreed that if ever a writer made an indel-
ible mark on his time, if ever anyone could be said to
have given the lead to the most important movements
of his day, Erasmus was that man. There are some
aspects of his world not reflected in his work; but
there are few, if any, of his leading ideas which did
not sow themselves far and wide and penetrate into
the very lives and mental outlook of his contemporaries.
He stands at the fountain-head of that spate of ideas
which flooded northern Europe in the early sixteenth
century; and every person who could read, from the
schoolboy to the theologian, was bound to imbibe his
notions and become conscious of his attitude of mind.
Sometimes this consciousness resulted in violent protest and enmity, but Erasmus was always a force to
be reckoned with, to enemies as well as friends.

It will lead us to know him better if we attempt to
analyse the extent to which he was in agreement with
his time, as it looks to us now, and to what extent he
rose beyond and above it as all great minds do. And
on the way we may come to form some generalisations
about the time itself, that much discussed and over-
defined Renaissance, which has been seen by some
historians as a New Era and a clean break with the
past, and by others—more modern—as the final stage
of a continuous process which stretches far back into
the Middle Ages. To these, Nordström in particular,
it is a wild error to think of the Renaissance as having
any characteristics of suddenness or violent change.
The fact that the sixteenth-century humanist thought
of himself as turning his back on the past, as reinstating

an ideal of civilisation long lost to humanity, illustrates for them the incapacity of an epoch to judge itself aright. No doubt there is much truth in this. It remains true, however, that to men like Erasmus or Ronsard their time seemed more like revolution than evolution : they rejoiced in its divergence from the immediate past.

Again, to some the Renaissance means the enfranchisement of the human spirit, the shaking-off of the age-long dictatorship of medieval theology, the freeing of energies that could now be concentrated on science and the investigation of the material world, rousing a new spirit of self-confidence and hope. To others it is the beginning of the great mistake, the era which first dared to place Man in the centre of a universe which had hitherto seemed to revolve round the conception of God (until by a turn of the wheel Science was to relegate Man to a station humbler than any dreamt of by theology). If we are to take Erasmus as typical of his age, it will become clear that neither of these opposing views is fully true. Again, the Renaissance has been considered as essentially an æsthetic and artistic revival, and to consist primarily in the acquisition of a sense of form; or on the other hand, it has been seen more intellectually as a fundamental change in outlook, the acquisition of a sense of history, or at any rate of increased self-realisation and historical perspective. These two conceptions may seem unrelated but they are not mutually exclusive: they both present the Renaissance as a kind of parallel to the adolescence of a single human being, in which the consciousness of self is sufficiently developed to allow the person in question to stand outside himself and

consider his own character and history, against the
background of the Not-Self which he perceives clearly
for the first time. This is perhaps the most widely
acceptable view of the Renaissance, and it accounts
for the prevailing passion for classical antiquity: it was
the revelation of a more mature civilisation, and the
comparison of medieval Europe with it, that shocked
the man of the fifteenth and sixteenth centuries into
self-consciousness. To northern Europe there was a
secondary pole of comparison, the Italy of the painters
and humanists, and in many of the French writers of
the sixteenth century the mention of Italy is accompanied by a sense of inferiority and spirit of emulation
which irresistibly suggests youth.

It is not suggested that any great answers to this
long struggle for a definition of the Renaissance will
be found in this little book. But from discussing the
subject with Erasmus, who certainly appeared to his
century as a living definition of Humanism, we shall
at least hope to find out what he thought he was doing,
what the discovery of the antique world meant to him,
and how far he himself recognised continuity between
his ideals and those of the past. We may also be
emboldened to ask him even deeper questions, and
discover whether he has any message for ourselves
unperceived by his own generation.

If, as Montaigne said, we were able to call on the
great Erasmus, and join the throng of acquaintances
that freely sought his door, we could not do better than
choose the year 1521. In that summer he was living
at Anderlecht, now a suburb of Brussels. The house
where he stayed, then the home of a canon of St.
Peter's church named Wychman, is still standing

to-day (or was when the present writer was privileged
to visit it in 1933). The portion occupied by Erasmus
was taken down about a hundred years ago, but there
remains a modest house, standing in a leafy garden,
in the quiet neighbourhood of a Béguinage. Passing
through the garden to the door, one enters the world
of the Renaissance; sixteenth-century furniture stands
in the low-ceilinged rooms, and casements open on the
cool greenness of a secluded garden, and in the hall
a scholar's gown and soft square cap hang negligently
on a peg, suggesting that the distinguished visitor has
just come in from the after-dinner walk he liked. On
the fringe of a great industrial city this oasis of calm
brings one both physically and spiritually into contact
with the past.

From Erasmus's letters and portraits we can form
a clear picture of what we should have found, if we had
knocked on that door in August 1521. We should no
doubt have been admitted readily, for Erasmus was
no recluse. Probably we should have found him sitting
at his table, a man of just over fifty, wearing perhaps
even in summer one of the fur-lined gowns of the
portraits, with his curly fair hair, now turning grey,
escaping from under his square cap; we should recognise the calm eyes looking out from a thin face
already lined, the firm straight mouth betraying both
sensitivity and humour, and on the long delicate
fingers touching the books piled before him, the gleam
of rings. The room might resemble the study in which
he was sketched in 1530, comfortably furnished according to the ideas of the time; chairs with elaborately
carved arms, a table standing on solid end-pieces
adorned with grotesque animal heads, the walls hung

with tapestries in an arabesque design, the windows framed by pilasters with carved capitals. A cupboard standing open would reveal shelves of books in clasped bindings. On the table, inkpots, hour-glass, book-rests and a slender vase of flowers; opposite to the humanist a young secretary or servant-pupil, writing.

The slight figure which rose to meet us would be that of the most famous man in Europe, but the interview would not be difficult or awe-inspiring, for Erasmus had the gift of making friends. We should probably have fallen under his charm, while he told us of his pleasure in finding this summer retreat in the country, in planning to come back here every year; of how he had thought country life was over-estimated until this experience had convinced him of the contrary. In a letter written from Anderlecht he describes how he fell ill in the town, and his whole life was a discussion with doctors and a succession of potions, powders, ointments, baths and plasters, and there was no time to be ill anyway. So he packed up his luggage and got on his horse. The servant inquired where he was going. "Anywhere," said Erasmus, "where the climate is healthy and kind." After two days in the country at Anderlecht the fever left him, and he felt himself growing young again.

This month of August was a happy one for him. It was during that month in 1521, that he went to Bruges to attend, as an Imperial Councillor, on the Emperor Charles V; and to take part in the interview between the Emperor and Cardinal Wolsey, who had come over from England on a diplomatic mission, to draw England and Spain together in league against France. In Wolsey's train were many of Erasmus's

English friends, including Thomas More; and about the Imperial court he met some of the great, including the King of Denmark who showed him much kindness and attention. Erasmus, the illegitimate son of a priest, born in obscurity, could not help liking importance and flattery: it measured the long distance which he had travelled in his amazing life. But he had also a flair for true character, and it was in these weeks at Anderlecht that he wrote a short biography of his friend Colet, the Dean of St. Paul's, and the least worldly of men, which showed his deep love and respect for disinterested and saintly learning. He wrote also a letter to Budé describing the household of Thomas More, not forgetting certainly that More had recently accepted a high post at the Court of Henry VIII, but also dwelling lovingly on More's simplicity and love of learning, and his success in the teaching of his children. More's daughters had all written to him in their faultless Latin.

Through his many friendships, and the wide correspondence he maintained with scholars in all parts of Europe, Erasmus had links with most countries of the continent; but at this time his situation was peculiar—they were all angling for his presence. During 1521 and 1522, he was approached from France, from Italy, from Switzerland. Francis I desired to add his presence as an ornament to a brilliant court, and Budé and many others constituted themselves spokesmen for the King. He was invited to Rome, where a majority of the Cardinals favoured his opinions, and the same rich libraries and hospitable palaces lay open to him as he had already enjoyed in 1509. Henry VIII had long promised him favours if he would return to

England, where he had so many friends. Zwingli begged him to visit Zurich and receive the freedom of the city. But Erasmus, as he replied in September 1522, preferred to be a citizen of the world, or perhaps rather a pilgrim. And he added, if only one could as easily enrol oneself as a freeman of the City of God!

The once obscure Augustinian canon might have turned anywhere in Europe, and been acclaimed as a prince of learning doing honour to the country which received him. A glance at his reputation and the work on which it rested will explain the reasons for this ascendancy over the minds of his generation.

In 1521, Erasmus was financially independent, owing to the stipend he had held as Imperial Councillor since 1516, and pensions derived from benefices. But all his life he had clung to his personal freedom, in spite of difficulties and struggles, and had refused to hold any post which could interfere with his wholehearted attachment to learning. The longest period for which he had held a teaching post was the two years spent at Cambridge from 1511–13 as Lady Margaret Professor of Greek. The results of this jealously guarded independence were so many and various as to secure him a European reputation in a number of fields.

By 1521, he was known as an editor, translator and populariser of the classics; as the editor and translator of the New Testament and the Fathers; as the most witty and penetrating satirist of his time; as a writer with new and startling ideas on social and religious questions. If his works up to that date could have been assembled in the study at Anderlecht, they would have represented a large part of the contemporary reading of an educated person. Editions of the classics and translations from the Greek, including Aristotle, Lucian, Plutarch, Euripides, Seneca, and many others, would have appeared on the shelves side by side with studies in educational methods and school-books, under titles such as *A Method of Study*, *The Teaching of Children*, *Letter-Writing*, *On Fluency*. There would have been a Latin translation of Gaza's Greek grammar, and the enthusiastic Platonic dialogue of Erasmus's youth, the *Book against the Barbarians*. Above all, his massive volume of the Adages, collected from a vast array of classical writers, the cream of the wisdom of antiquity. But a larger section of his library would have held his contribution to religious thought: the Handbook of a Christian soldier (*Enchiridion Militis Christiani*) that wonderful little masterpiece of good sense and deep faith; editions of Valla's *Annotations* on the New Testament, and many of the Fathers, including Ambrose, Augustine, Chrysostom, Jerome; above all, his first edition of the New Testament in Greek, with a new Latin translation beside it, and a set of Paraphrases on the Epistles (the *Paraphrases of the Gospels*, in 1521, are lying on the humanist's table in process of completion).

Turning to another side of his library, we should find the books which set all Europe laughing: his *Colloquies*, begun long before as a school-book, and now reappearing year by year in expanded form (Erasmus loved dialogues, and here all his contemporaries live and move like actors crossing a stage); and *The Praise of Folly*, that enigmatic little book, tossed off in a day or two at Thomas More's house in London, and so greedily devoured by public taste that forty editions were issued during the author's own life. His meditations on social questions are scattered throughout his books, especially the last two mentioned, and touch many sides of life, from questions which have always been controversial, such as the existence of war, and the position of women, to those debated particularly in his own day, such as the merits and demerits of the monastic life. On some topics he wrote essays, such as the one *In Praise of Marriage* and the book on Confession (*Exomologesis*). But his most important work on government was his *Education of a Christian Prince*, written three years after Machiavelli's *Prince* and revealing a very different notion of statesmanship.

The publications of Erasmus up to 1521 would in fact have made a compact little library and in themselves provided a liberal education for the use of his generation. No wonder that his contemporaries looked on him with admiration and wonder, writing to him "*suavissime praeceptor . . . splendidissime vir . . .*" or like John Watson in 1516: "I marvel more and more to see how Erasmus as he advances in years advances in greatness, revealing himself every day in a new and fuller light." And when Rabelais, writing to Erasmus near the end of his master's life, speaks of him as the source of all the knowledge and inspiration of his time, one feels that Rabelais (here as elsewhere) is speaking not for himself alone but for the Renaissance.

One word more to complete our portrait of Erasmus in 1521; the storm of the Reformation, which was to sadden the end of Erasmus's life, was rising, but it had not yet enveloped Europe in a cloud of acrimony, persecution and civil war. Luther had been in open revolt for four years, and in January, 1521, was excommunicated for heresy. By May he was in the protective custody of the Wartburg, and banned, himself and all his works, from the territories of the Empire. Erasmus, painfully aware of the danger of schism, disapproving of Luther's violence and intransigence, but sympathising with him on many points, steadily refused to take sides against him. Later on he would feel compelled to do so; but in 1521 he still hoped to stand aside from the *mêlée*, find peace from his enemies (who were also Luther's) and go on uninterrupted with his task of portraying to the world the ideal of wisdom, simplicity and practical goodness which he called the Philosophy of Christ.

All the essentials of Erasmus's life are thus clearly to be seen in 1521: his leadership in his century's *ruée vers l'or*, the rediscovery of the classics; his shrewd perception of values and his sense of reality; his individualistic attitude to religion, combining a reasoning knowledge of the Scriptures with a simple devotion which led him to the threshold of mysticism; his strong interest in the conduct of the world's affairs; his refusal to join a party or enrol himself under any banner, or to accept any ready-made solution to the problems of the spirit; his hatred of war. So, representative but individualistic, he stands out against the background of his age. His generation recognised him as its own expression, especially in his sense of personal freedom. The example he set in bringing all questions to the bar of the individual conscience, and turning the light of the intellect on to customs and prejudices cobwebbed with the acquiescence of ages, was to play a great part in the growth of rationalism in Europe.

The importance of his work in this direction was so great that it was natural for people to forget his more positive side. In his reliance on individual judgment as against accepted tradition, he seemed to prepare the way for Descartes; in his sceptical attitude to dogma and philosophy he was akin to Montaigne. For many generations it was the destructive power of his gay intellect which impressed his readers, accustomed to think of him above all as the author of *The Praise of Folly*. But in our own time a rather different view of Erasmus is coming to the fore. As the result of the tireless labours of a number of scholars, it is now becoming more possible to see him as a whole, and to judge his mind not only from the brilliant flashes of satiric insight which it threw off from time to time like sparks, but from the quieter and more fundamental parts of his huge literary output. From this emerges a much more positive ideal than has usually been credited to Erasmus.

Even to his contemporaries there is no doubt that he appeared to be an attacker rather than a builder. For that passionate age his ideal was a difficult one to understand and it tended to become obscured behind the qualities which his contemporaries could recognise as being their own. When that ideal led him to refuse to take sides in their internecine struggles, they accused him of cowardice and easy compromise. The truth was that in his resolute detachment from their conflicts, he must have been both admirable and exasperating for his age. It is not enough to say that he advocated compromise; he simply failed to see the

xxii

necessity for some of the fiercest struggles which divided his generation. His practical common sense rendered him immune from them. For instance, the revival of classical thought appeared to many serious-minded people as incompatible with a belief in the supreme revelation of Christ; to Erasmus the question is simply resolved by an acceptance of all in the ancient world which is in harmony with Christian thought, and he sums up the position with an unruffled: *Sancte Socrates, ora pro nobis.* Again Luther accused Erasmus of drawing back after having preached independence of thought, because Erasmus said it was unwise to expect all and sundry to debate complicated problems of theology. The question at issue was fundamental to the Reformation: was religious doctrine and philosophy to be the domain of a class of experts, as had been mainly the case during the Middle Ages, or was each man to be his own priest and interpreter of the Scriptures? Erasmus, the translator of the New Testament, had been one of the first to say that truth should be within reach of all, that intellect was given to each man for use in the service of God. But to Luther he says that one can go too far in vulgarising theology; although the simple in heart may be nearer to a mystical understanding of the Divine, when it comes to a rational discussion there are some truths so far above our grasp that it is useless, if not harmful, to debate them in public and bandy words on subjects that the deepest thinkers find beyond them. So, many a time, Erasmus infuriated the slower-witted of his contemporaries by not being the slave of logic, and refusing to push to a final conclusion any of the theories he promulgated for the reformation of his world.

He was essentially practical, and impatient of abstract reasoning; his aim was to find his way to the good life, and theories and doctrines were judged by their contribution to this end.

This deliberate aloofness from intellectual controversy is seen best of all in his attitude to the question nearest the heart of the Renaissance, that of the value of Man and all his works. Erasmus contributed perhaps more than anyone to the rebirth of confidence in the innate powers of the human mind. The spirit which animated the early adventurers was fostered by him in ways of learning; no sea was to be unnavigable in the world of thought. In seeing the future clear for the triumphant expansion of the mind of man, he was a true humanist. But to the Humanism which imagines Man as supreme lord of the universe, needing no God to inspire and no Christ to redeem him, Erasmus was a stranger; that intoxicated celebration of human potentialities which gave its glitter to the Italian Renaissance was foreign to his mind. He did not even ask those questions which were to inspire the deep rift which soon widened between Humanists and Reformers; to argue about whether Man were all or God were all would have seemed to him as unnecessary as the hair-splitting discussions of the Schoolmen. So between the Italian humanist with his faith in mankind and his views "on all things knowable," and the Calvinist with his determination to regard all the works of man, not founded on Faith, as so many sins, stands Erasmus, sure that the works of man, in so far as they are good, are the works of God, and that human wisdom is inspired and finally crowned by the revelation of the Divine.

It is this refreshing common sense, and the serene and simple ideal of life which it helped to produce, which attracts us in Erasmus now. He is no longer a sceptic for us; his middle way holds some answers to our own seeking. And yet one must not go too far in setting him up as a leader of thought; he would have found that very unlikely and amusing. He was the reverse of pompous, and the fascination of his personality lies in his sincerity, his humour, his ready sympathies, in being in fact so human; and perhaps (as P. S. Allen suggests in a delightful essay),[1] in the lingering traditional recollection that we have of him as the enchanting conversationalist, "the Master of those who talk."

[1] *Erasmus*, Oxford, 1934.

Chapter One

The Legacy of the Past

ERASMUS was born into a world which was rapidly changing, and in this respect his experience is easily entered into by the reader of the twentieth century. He was born to an inheritance of old and settled beliefs, a mental attitude once universally shared, but already menaced and falling into disrepute. During his lifetime a revolution was accomplished, and in some ways it was parallel to that accomplished during the lifetime of any Englishman born in 1876 and living till 1936; though, of course, in some respects it was the exact reverse. The change in religious outlook has some similarities in the two epochs; a period of dogmatism, of outward observances and general acceptance of a basic creed, giving place to a period of liberation from authority, uncertain seeking and wide divergences of belief. In other ways perhaps, there is a kinship of opposites between the two epochs: in Erasmus's day the local self-government of town and guild, the regional autonomy of the great vassals, was accomplishing the last phase of its evolution towards political centralisation of power in the hands of a monarch, while to us who live in the twentieth century the fall of monarchies has become a commonplace, and the communal view of society is again becoming dominant.

We have seen also, the end of that pre-eminence in

education of Greek and Latin studies, the introduction of which was one of the marked characteristics of the Renaissance. When Rabelais, in *Gargantua*, hit off the difference brought about in education in his time, he may have been exaggerating a little, but if Erasmus had had the time or the inclination to read a frivolous French book he would no doubt have smiled in assent. But the causes underlying this change, if examined, point to the real likeness and dissimiliarity between the two epochs. In our own day immense changes in point of view, even in the situation of mankind on the planet, have been brought about by the hitherto unimaginable development of science and the machine. In Erasmus's day a similar change in point of view, perhaps in its way as shattering and as profound, was taking place owing to the invention of printing. This early intervention of the machine in our affairs was largely in favour of the New Learning, so that the enlarged horizon offered by the classics stood to the men of the Renaissance in much the same relationship as the discoveries of the physicists of the twentieth century to the general public today, affording a breath-taking glimpse into a new kind of reality.

Of that educational change Erasmus was one of the prime artificers, as also, not altogether willingly, of the religious revolution. Of the political changes happening round him, he was a spectator only, and not always in sympathy with the new trends. He was enough a man of his time to accept the principle of monarchy as the normal foundation for society, but he was anxious to hedge it in with moral sanctions which should preserve the liberty of the people, highly important in his eyes. Was he influenced in this by his childhood in Holland? There is very little trace of any nationalistic feeling in Erasmus's writings, but much of the reverse, a cosmopolitanism of the intellect unequalled except by Voltaire; and there are only a few signs of affectionate feeling for his native country. Perhaps he became more favourably inclined to it as he grew older, farther away from his unhappy and frustrated youth, more able to appreciate its virtues. Certainly his chief anxiety for many years was to keep away from it, and some of its characteristics represented for him the very antithesis of his own tastes. Yet in spite of this antipathy, it is possible to trace some of the deepest preoccupations of his life to his early education in Holland.

The Holland of Erasmus's childhood was a scene of busy traffic, commercial prosperity, and political unrest. Of the seventeen states later to be unified as the United Provinces, eleven had been drawn together under the rule of the Dukes of Burgundy, Philip the Good and his successor, Charles the Bold. The mid-fifteenth century had seen a magnificent outlay of wealth and luxury at the courts of Burgundy, and the rich towns of the Netherlands had been the subsoil for the flowering of Dutch and Flemish art. But the ambitions of Charles the Bold, dreaming of a Burgundian kingdom, had been quietly demolished by the crafty planning of Louis XI, and the death of Charles in 1477, leaving no heir but his daughter Mary, allowed the scheming King to round off his domains by adding Burgundy to France. Under Mary and her husband Maximilian, the Netherlands were never at peace, and not till they were taken over in 1492 by Mary's son Philip the Fair was there any cessation of civil war. This period of anarchy and devastation coincided with Erasmus's later schooldays and experience of monastic life in the convent of Steyn. It was no wonder that Holland was associated in his mind on the one hand with gross material pleasures such as drinking and feasting, on the other with boorishness and lack of intellectual standards. Like most people who react violently against their early environment, and live through a great transition, he tended to minimise the inheritance of his youth.

In any case Erasmus could never have been happy to remain in his native country, because of the circumstances of his birth. Living elsewhere, he could surround them with a romantic mystery, could even veil them altogether in the blaze of his fame. But in Gouda or Rotterdam they were not to be forgotten.

The facts are only known to us through Erasmus himself, and the allusions of a few contemporaries whose stories are hard to reconcile with each other. Erasmus's own accounts, one written in 1516 as a letter to a papal secretary,[1] and the other in 1524 in his *Compendium Vitae*,[2] are both documents with a purpose. The first is an appeal to the Pope for remission of the disabilities which illegitimacy entailed (for instance, legal incapacity to hold benefices) and for permission to live outside the monastery. The second is an attempt to place his father and mother in the best possible light. Both strike the reader as pathetic, the first in its urgency to be delivered from a situation which uncertainty made intolerable, the second in its laconic, staccato phrases, dealing rapidly with a distasteful subject. It is clear that Erasmus's life

[1] Allen, *Erasmi Epistolae*, II, 447.   [2] Allen, I, p. 46.

was darkened and harassed by the memory of his youth.

From the two accounts we can derive a number of basic facts which there is no reason to doubt. His father Gerard was a priest of the neighbourhood of Gouda, his mother Margaret, the daughter of a physician called Peter, of Severnbergen. In an early brief from the Pope (Julius II) to Erasmus in 1506,[1] the relationship is said to have been one between a bachelor and a widow, but in 1516 the new dispensation refers to it as not only an illegitimate connection but "as he fears, an incestuous and accursed" one, meaning that the father was already a priest. The gravity of the issue depended on this alone: was Erasmus's father already in orders when his son was born? In his later account, well-known to English readers through Charles Reade's use of it in *The Cloister and the Hearth*, Erasmus spins what one biographer calls "a web of romance" round this question, describing his father's parents, Elias and Catherine and their ten sons, of whom Gerard was the youngest but one, and how in order to obtain his part of the inheritance the brothers united to force Gerard into the priesthood. Before his ordination he had a secret love affair with Margaret, in the hope of marriage; and his son adds, "and some say that they were formally betrothed" (*intercessisse verba*). The opposition of the family, however, drove Gerard to leave home, and he went to Rome, where he supported himself by copying manuscripts and became a Latin and Greek scholar. These manuscripts became the patrimony of his sons, and we may imagine the young

[1] See Allen, II, p. 434.

Erasmus's feelings on turning them over in later years. But the treachery of Gerard's brothers, who sent him word that Margaret was dead, drove him to take orders, and on his return home he kept his vows and never lived with her again.

A gallant story: is it invalidated by the fact that here Erasmus does not mention the existence of his brother Peter, three years older than himself? In the other account of his youth Peter is fully in the picture, and Erasmus's early letters testify to their continued relations during adolescence. Probably the truth is that while it was wishful thinking on Erasmus's part to lay stress on the serious "hope of marriage," yet, having been born during his father's absence in Rome, he could never be quite sure whether or not his father was in orders at the actual time of his birth. And it is perhaps significant that the older he grew, the farther back he tended to push his birth-year, so that from his own allusions it is not possible to decide conclusively when he was born. The probabilities lie between the years 1466 and 1469, with perhaps a bias in favour of 1469. Clearly, the farther back he could place his own birth, the greater the likelihood of its having taken place while his father was a young bachelor and free from vows of celibacy. The only certainty we have is that Erasmus kept the eve of S.S. Simon and Jude (October 27th) as his birthday.

The irregularity of his birth did not deprive him of parental care. He is said to have been born at Rotterdam, but spent the first years of his childhood at Gouda, where he went to the school kept by Peter Winckel, afterwards one of his guardians. By his own report he was a dull scholar in "those unbeautiful

6

studies for which he was not born," presumably the Dutch language. At the age of nine or thereabouts his father sent him to the famous school of St. Lebwin's at Deventer, and his mother accompanied him there, "as the guardian and nurse of his tender years." Here Erasmus came under the influence of the chief educational movement in the Low Countries, and as his whole childhood and adolescence was spent in this atmosphere, in contact with an ideal of life which roused his opposition at the time but had its deep effect on his character, it is important to examine for a moment the nature of this movement.

The school of Deventer was attached to the great church of St. Lebwin's; but the teachers were not necessarily all ecclesiastics. Many of them belonged to the community of the Brethren of the Common Life, a lay society which was already nearly a hundred years old. It had been founded by the disciples of Gerard Groote (b. 1384), himself a native of Deventer, who had drunk deep of the learning of his time before turning to the Bible and the Fathers and coming under the influence of the mystic Ruysbroeck. During the lifetime of Groote certain beginnings of community life had shown themselves; he had turned his own house into a refuge for women penitents, and had gathered together a circle of poor students, who lived a monastic life and spent their time in transcribing manuscripts. But it was his intimate friend, Florent Radewijns, who became the founder of the first community, parent of many others which spread out into the towns of the Low Countries. Both men and women joined them, living in separate communities on the monastic model but still in the world, bound by no eternal vows but associated by a common ideal of simplicity and poverty, and putting their daily earnings into a common purse. On Sundays and holy days they preached to the people, using the simple language of everyday life; their mission was essentially a practical and public one. But they were in no way opposed to the monastic ideal, and Groote, on his deathbed, had confided to Radewijns his dream of founding a monastery where the life of contemplation as he knew it might be led apart from the world. The result of his dream was the Abbey of Windesheim, and by the time of Erasmus's boyhood a whole complex of monasteries and convents were living and working in harmony with the free communities of the Brethren.

These parallel developments had great significance in the religious life of northern Europe. In the main they represent two trends of thought and feeling: on the one hand a revulsion from the sterile intellectual disputes of late-medieval philosophy, a reorientation towards practical piety and the teaching of the Bible; on the other, a widespread attempt to reform the monastic orders, which has its clearest manifestation in the foundation of Windesheim. Their spokesman, listened to throughout the ages, is known to us as Thomas à Kempis. In the *Imitation of Christ* their authentic, unmistakable voice may still be heard, urging the value of an ascetic life, not as a discipline so much as a way to the experience of the love of God; exposing with delicate acuteness the vagaries of human self-interest; exalting obedience and self-renunciation, and above all humility, the contempt of worldly honours, the patient acceptance of injuries,

8

the quiet fulfilment of humbler tasks; and expressing suspicion and mistrust towards the pride of worldly learning. The goal of human life is spiritual communion with God, absorption in the love of Christ, and the only road to this end is through utter abnegation of self. No more formidable obstacle to this exists than intellectual pride. So again and again in the pages of the *Imitation* the warnings recur, raising for us the spectre of the barren learning of the schools, the hair-splitting on trivial questions or the web-spinning of philosophical and theological speculation of which Thomas was thinking as he wrote: "Of what advantage is it to dispute profoundly about the doctrine of the Trinity, if by your lack of humility you are all the while displeasing the Trinity? I would rather feel compunction than know how to define it. If you knew the whole Bible, and the maxims of all the philosophers, what would it profit you if you were destitute of the love of God and of His grace?"

This attitude is expressed clearest of all in the chapter entitled "Against vain and worldly learning" (III, 43). "I am the One who teaches men knowledge, and I impart to little ones a clearer knowledge than can be taught by man ... I in a moment can lift up the humble mind, and make it enter more deeply into the principles of Eternal Truth, than if one had studied ten years in the schools."

This, then, was a predominant note in the early education of Erasmus—a deep distrust of the powers of the intellect. A strange beginning for a humanist of the Renaissance! In later life the influence of this early teaching shows itself in his thought; but in his boyhood he was in quest of far different things.

Into his northern dyke-land floated rumours of what was happening in the far south: the rediscovery of the ancient world which was the work of the Italian humanists, who ever since the time of Petrarch and Boccaccio had been collecting manuscripts, forming libraries, investigating the traces of ancient Rome, exploring the lost world of Greek culture. No attempt can be made here to describe the glories of the Italian Renaissance, but we may recall that the youth of Erasmus coincided with the fullest activity of the Platonic Academy of Florence, the circle of *littérateurs* round Lorenzo de Medici, the greatest of them being Marsilio Ficino, whose great translation of Plato was begun in 1463. In that year also Ficino's most noted disciple was born. No greater contrast to the ascetic principles of the Brethren could be imagined, than is seen in the person of Pico della Mirandola, young, precocious, brilliant, plunging with enthusiasm into his task of combining antique philosophy and widely-culled learning with Christian belief, and giving his treatises titles like *De omni scibili* and *De dignitate hominis*. Pico's works have been relegated to the limbo of erudition, but in their time they embodied the vigorous intellectual curiosity and the faith in humanity characteristic of the Renaissance.

Erasmus was never interested in the ramifications of philosophy, nor, apparently, in the flowering of Renaissance art, though he lived through its best period: in that year when he probably went first to Deventer (1475) Michael Angelo was born. But from the first he was passionately anxious to explore the world in which both were rooted, the hitherto uncharted realm of classical antiquity. Italy to him was not so much the soil of a new springtime of culture, a new artistic revival, as the home of scholars and philologists, a place where classical manuscripts could still be unearthed, where the study of Greek was common, where thanks to the untiring labours of devoted men the great vision of the antique world was slowly becoming clear, a breathlessly beautiful inheritance to be grasped at by his own generation. The sense of this vision never left him, though it was not with a blind devotion that he embraced the past. Throughout his life he looked to the wisdom of the classical world for all the secular education his own world needed, and saw no antagonism between the highest ideals of antiquity and the teaching of Christ.

This enthusiasm dated from his boyhood, and was fostered in the somewhat inclement atmosphere of the schools of Deventer and Bois-le-Duc. When Erasmus looked back forty years later, from a world so greatly enriched, and to a large extent by his own efforts, he thought those schools ignorant and barbarous. At Deventer the boys learnt Latin from elementary tables of declensions and then from the versified grammars in fashion at the time, incorrect and time-wasting. These were read aloud to classes which must have numbered 200 or more, and the scholars wrote down what they could catch in the notebooks which were their only classbooks. Erasmus did not progress quickly by this method, and when he left Deventer, he was only in the third class. One may imagine him as a bright boy with an inkling of better things, impatiently scornful of a method of instruction which offered nothing but false etymologies and diffuse definitions of terms, when what he pined for was to be introduced to poetry and history and thought, the great storehouse of untouched treasure to which Latin was the golden key.

But like many other schoolboys, he found his encouragement indirectly. He must have had access to some books, for we are told that he learnt by heart the whole of the plays of Terence. (One is reminded of Montaigne, whose tutor wisely pretended not to know that his pupil was devouring Ovid, Virgil and Terence in secret, and thus preserved to them the delicious taste of forbidden fruit.) If Erasmus's own teachers were dull, there were others in the school who were aware of the new trends in learning: one of the teachers, John Sintheim, was a friend of the famous scholar Rudolph Agricola, who came to visit the school when Erasmus was there. Before he left a new headmaster, Alexander Hegius, was to infuse new life into the teaching. After his time the schools of the Brethren of the Common Life welcomed more and more the ideas of the humanists, and numbered among their pupils many of the best scholars of the Low Countries. It seems as if Hegius and his friends reconciled in their minds two very different ideals, the humble striving after the good life recommended by Thomas à Kempis and the exaltation of knowledge and eloquence learnt from the Italian humanists. There are traces in Erasmus of this duality, and he may well have received some encouragement at the close of his school career from the more scholarly of his teachers. There is indeed a story of Sintheim embracing the boy with the words "Courage, Erasmus, one day you will reach the highest peak of learning," and dismissing him with a kiss. But Sintheim taught

12

only in the higher classes, and Hegius Erasmus only heard on feast days when he spoke to the assembled school.

Erasmus describes himself at this time as swept onwards towards the New Learning by a hidden and overpowering instinct: *occulta naturae vi rapiebar ad bonas literas*. His destiny was clear from the beginning and there was no turning him from it. In many ways this passion for learning was, as we have seen, contrary to the ideals of his earliest environment: and yet in his later life the effect of early religious teaching can be traced, and some important elements in his attitude to life he actually shared with the Brethren. Like them he hated theorising and abstract speculation, the kind of intellectual pride which is based on faultless logic. Like them he had a turn for the practical, and came early to the conclusion that the goal of all learning is the good life, and that the way to it lies in the study of Scripture, though in his youth the fascination of classical literature had somewhat dimmed this truth. And though he enjoyed fame and distinction, humility of character remained for him the finest quality a man can have; how often in his letters an enthusiastic description of a friend contains the word "modest" as essential praise!

The end of his stay at Deventer was brought about by tragic circumstances and ushered in the most painful period of his life.[1] Plague was sweeping the Low Countries, and his mother, who had accompanied him to Deventer, died of it. Erasmus was then, he tells us, aged thirteen. The house in which he boarded was emptied by the plague, and the boy

[1] See Allen, I, Appendix I. Hyma, *The Youth of Erasmus*.

returned to Gouda, where his father also died in a very short time. He tells us that he was not much more than fourteen when he was left an orphan, under the care of three guardians, of whom the chief was Peter Winckel, the schoolmaster of Gouda.

* * *

Looking back on his youth from a time when his European fame had justified all his early struggles, Erasmus was severe in his judgments on those who had failed to appreciate or direct his adolescent mind. He tells the story at great length in his letter to "Grunnius," (apparently an imaginary Papal secretary) and as his letter is designed to show that his entry into the monastic life had been forced on him by circumstances, he perhaps darkens the picture. However, the story he tells is in no way incredible or even unlikely, and something like it must have happened. After his return from Deventer, Erasmus and his brother were sent to another school taught by the Brethren of the Common Life at 's Hertogenbosch (or Bois-le-Duc). Here they stayed for two years, and as the school was less progressive than the Deventer one Erasmus considered those years entirely wasted. The question of settlement in life was now looming up, and the boys found that everyone round them was working hard to influence them towards the monastic life. There had always been a tendency for the schools of the Brethren of the Common Life to train boys for the religious orders; in Erasmus's view that was their chief aim. (He regretted in later life that he had not joined the Brethren then and there; at least he would not have taken irrevocable

14

vows.) On returning to Gouda, the boys found that Peter Winckel was virtually their only tutor, as one of the others was dead, and the third, a banker, had lost interest in them. And Peter Winckel was also of opinion that the monastic life held their best future. Here were two illegitimate boys, debarred by their birth from holding preferment in the Church, with no family and very little money (Erasmus throws out dark hints as to mismanagement of their small patrimony). Around them was political insecurity, social misery and unrest. It was small wonder then, if the schoolmaster longed to rid himself of his embarrassing function by settling them both in monastic houses for a peaceful, secure and uneventful life.

It was true that the younger had troublesome ideas. Several clear glimpses of the adolescent Erasmus are offered about this time. Failure to take him seriously still rankled in his mind, as he went over it all thirty years later. The first letter of his that we have was apparently written when he was still a boy, urging Peter Winckel to proceed in the sale of some books (probably the MSS. which constituted his father's legacy). The schoolmaster, nettled by the tone and the style (the young cock quoted Ovid!), replied dryly that next time Erasmus wrote a letter like that, he should add a commentary. There was little sympathy there for a budding scholar, and Erasmus's one idea was to get away. He recalls conversations with his brother, in which Peter confessed that not religious fervour, but fear of their tutor, inclined him to give way and enter the monastery. Erasmus succeeded in firing his brother with enough courage to resist, and they attempted to present a united front, declaring that they wished to go to a University before taking a decision involving their entire lives. Brave words, but after a storm of rage the tutor tried friendly persuasion, and Peter was not proof against the change of tone. He accepted the offer of a canonry in the monastery of Sion, near Delft, and Erasmus was left to resist alone.

He held out for a time, and recalled it as the most wretched period of his life. Where could a boy turn, completely alone, inexperienced and ill of a recurrent fever, when all around him were by one consent working on his feelings? He recalled bitterly the childish stories they told him of the wickedness of the world, and the heavenly peace of the monastic life. So they laboured—Pharisees, he says, working so hard to bury alive one living and breathing boy. A chance meeting with a childhood friend, Cornelius of Woerden, brought him into contact with the monastery of Steyn, near Gouda, where Cornelius had taken refuge from poverty. Cornelius was interested in literature, and saw in Erasmus a companion who could help him with his studies. Together they worked far into the night (Erasmus remembered reading with him, in one night, a whole comedy of Terence). Here at last was congenial company, and Erasmus turned to Cornelius with all the affection of a sore and lonely and still childish heart. Soon he was living at Steyn, free to read to his heart's content; then remained as a novice, and describes himself as doing so under protest, giving way to the threats of his elders and the pleadings of Cornelius. The year's novitiate over, he was faced with the final step, and having no strength to break away

16

at that formidable point, found himself irrevocably a canon of Steyn.

Erasmus tells the story at great length, and it is coloured by his intense bitterness of feeling against the people and the institution which had clogged his progress and hampered his freedom of action. He may have felt less bitterly at the time than on looking back. But it is likely that he was aware from the beginning of his extreme physical unsuitability for the monastic life which he describes in his letter to "Grunnius," and that he was really unfitted for long fasts, broken nights, and the inhospitable climate of Steyn.

However, the step was taken: *Professus est.* Then followed in Erasmus's life a period of six years spent at the monastery, of which we can have only a general picture, derived from his surviving letters and from the views on monasticism he expressed in later years. That this period was not happy is fairly certain, that it was formative is certain too. It saw him pass from a sensitive, deeply shaken adolescence to the state of manhood and a clear purpose. To say that this development was favoured by the mental climate of Steyn would be untrue, but in the usual way of perverse mankind Erasmus was apparently confirmed in his purpose by the very obstructions which he had to surmount. He went into Steyn lonely, deserted by friends, emotionally overstrung, and we find him writing letters of passionate affection to another young monk, Servatius, who later was to become Prior of Steyn. Servatius was apparently irked or frightened by the force of feeling displayed, and thinking it contrary to the rules of his Order, received it coldly; or so we divine from Erasmus's letters, some of

17

which express deep dejection at the refusal of his friendship. Erasmus never published these letters himself; perhaps he was ashamed of them—but they express a very natural burst of adolescent feeling on the part of an intellectual and a poet. It is to be noted that the tone is soon modified into an appeal to Servatius not to desert the studies which were Erasmus's chief joy. From the beginning, to Erasmus, friendship was linked with learning: or perhaps it would be truer to say that it was a matter of breathing the same air, sharing the same atmosphere—the love of scholarship. A close and happy friendship with another young monk, William Herman, was permeated by this delight in the classics.

One survival testifies to an early attempt by Erasmus to adapt himself to the monastic ideal. This was a treatise *On the Contempt of the World*, written in the vein of Thomas à Kempis and perhaps intended to convince the author rather than the reader. In later years Erasmus practically disavowed this by adding a final chapter in which he criticises monasteries. But as it stood it was a faithful attempt to reproduce the teaching of the Brethren of the Common Life; and some of its observations, like the passage in which Erasmus speaks respectfully of the meditation of the mystic and says that he has only had a slight taste of it himself, express a fundamental attitude of his in later life.

Possibly this was written in the earlier part of his sojourn at Steyn. Other evidence points to an increasing determination to make his own way, to gain learning and be himself at all costs. We may surmise that as he developed, the certainty of having got into the wrong box grew clearer, and the very obstacles put in his way—the isolation, the constant interruptions, the difficulty of obtaining books, the rule against private property, the hostility of the brethren—all acted as a goad to urge him forward to the mastery and the freedom he sought.

A few friends were of inestimable value in the way of moral support. One was William Herman, the playfellow of his childhood and schooldays. Another was Cornelius Gerard of Gouda, older than Erasmus and like him an Augustinian Canon living at Hemsdonck near Gouda, or for a period at Lopsen, near Leiden. To him Erasmus wrote long letters deploring their forced separation, discussing literature, enclosing poems to be criticised, praising and defending his beloved author Lorenzo Valla, quoting Virgil, Terence, Horace, Martial. In one letter he gives a list of his favourite authors: "I have my masters, whom I follow; possibly you have different ones, and I shall not object to that. Mine are: in poetry Virgil, Horace, Ovid, Juvenal, Statius, Martial, Claudian, Persius, Lucan, Tibullus, Propertius; in prose Cicero, Quintilian, Sallust, Terence. And then as an authority on good writing I trust no one so much as Lorenzo Valla; we have no one to be compared to him in acuteness of mind and tenacity of memory. I confess that I should not dare to publish anything not authorised by these writings." In another letter he mentioned some of the scholars of his own time who seem to him to have reached the stature of the ancients: Hegius, his old schoolmaster, Rudolph Agricola, Aeneas Sylvius, Filelfo, Poggio, and others whose names have fallen into obscurity today. The unknown young monk in

Holland thinks of them with reverence, for as he says:
"I have and have had from a child, such a love of
Letters that they seem to me worthy to be preferred
before all the treasures of Arabia and all the wealth
of Crœsus." Another letter of this time describes the
state of depression in which he began his first work
of any importance, the *Book against the Barbarians*, a
dialogue in defence of good learning in a Platonic
setting.

Such a period of dejection was not natural to
Erasmus, and he was apparently planning to find a
way of escape and betake himself to a University,
when the doors of the monastery opened of their own
accord. Henry of Bergen, the Bishop of Cambrai,
was in expectation of becoming a cardinal and required a learned Secretary to accompany him to
Rome. Erasmus left the monastery to take up this post,
with the permission of his superiors, probably after
April 25th, 1492, when he was ordained priest by the
Bishop of Utrecht. Possibly his departure from the
monastery was as late as 1494. The Bishop took him
to his hereditary residence at Bergen-op-Zoom, where
he made a most valuable friend in the secretary to the
council of the town, James Batt; and in a period of
danger from plague, he followed the Bishop to his
country house at Halsteren. Little is known of this
part of Erasmus's life, except that the journey to Rome
proved to be a baseless vision. The Latin secretary of
the Bishop wondered what to do next, determined as
he was not to go back to the monastery. James Batt
said to him: "Why not ask the Bishop to send you to
study in Paris?" Erasmus clutched at the idea.

We have a few glimpses of his life and movements

at this time. One is afforded by the opening book of the *Antibarbari*. Here Erasmus describes his retirement to the country at Halsteren, the pastoral beauty of the setting and the health-giving air, and the little Academy he created for himself during the visit of William Herman. Together with James Batt the town clerk, the friends go for a walk and meet Jodocus, the doctor, and William Conrad, the mayor, and after bantering conversation fall to serious discussion. Their subject is the decline of true learning, and the reasons for its decline: and the discussion becomes finally a defence of classical learning and of poetry. When the book was published in 1520, Erasmus slightly altered it and inserted strong diatribes against the monasteries. But in the earliest version known these are absent, and what we find is a discussion on education and on what was to Erasmus the burning question of his time: What is true learning? Does it consist in getting by heart the Psalms, or learning Latin in the Book of Proverbs, or studying outmoded grammars; or is it opening a window on the world of history, philosophy and poetry? Is there, as people say, any danger in substituting pagan for Christian writers? Is Plato to be read instead of St. Thomas, and are boys to be given poetry and plays to read, Virgil and Terence, instead of works on scholastic theology? What will the result be in the lives of the next generation? Is a man more moral for being highly educated, or less so?

Erasmus was here meeting the great problem of his time: does secular learning contribute to spiritual growth or hinder it? In one form or another this has been a fundamental question in the history of mankind ever since the Renaissance. In our own day we see it in its most acute form, the terrifying query which makes uncertain the whole future of the human race. Knowledge divorced from moral values has progressed to such a point that unless a progression to a higher moral code accompanies it, man's mastery of the universe may be synonymous with his suicide. In Erasmus's day the problem had not assumed this magnitude, because scientific knowledge was in its infancy, and the "learning" which he was discussing had its human and moral side. But the question he was debating held the germ of all future developments. It was the question of the relation of learning to life.

Erasmus's views, as expressed by Batt in the dialogue, are, of course, strongly in defence of secular learning. In fighting the enemies of his cherished poets, he appears as a rationalist only, paying perfunctory lip-service to the wisdom of the heart so much praised by the teachers of his youth. At this time he was perhaps nearer to the Italian humanists, in their triumphant faith in reason, than ever again. Later on he was to modify his attitude, with greater understanding of the spiritual world. But at this time, sitting with his friends in the garden beside the clear stream, under the shade of the apple orchard in flower, he was much more of a poet and less of a devotional writer than he afterwards became. Divine inspiration? Well, of course nothing good can come without that—tha goes without saying—but what really matters just now to Erasmus is that young men like himself should be free to shake off the trammels of traditional education, laugh at the timorous taboos imposed by the clerical guides of the past, and plunge into the study of life itself, as represented by the great writers of Greece and Rome.

*   *   *

On arrival in Paris, it was as a poet that he introduced himself to the intellectual society there. Here, again, Erasmus must have found himself in a false position. He was now a priest, and had come to Paris to prepare for a degree in theology. For that purpose he entered the Collége de Montaigu, where the students led arduous and ascetic lives under their stern Rector, John Standonck, and conned over in their damp little rooms the notes they had taken from the lectures in logic or scholastic theology. Sometimes Erasmus would be invited to preach, perhaps in the great Abbey of Ste. Geneviève which crowned the hill on which Montaigu stood. He had contacts which linked him with his origins in the Low Countries, especially with the mission sent from Windesheim under John Mauburn to preach reform of the monasteries in Paris. Erasmus's youth had still a strong hold upon him. And yet how ardently he was desiring and struggling towards a different kind of life, towards fame and friends of his own making!

Paris was a *pis aller* to the humanist who had prepared for a journey to Rome. Instead of treading that sacred soil now bursting into a second flowering of scholarship and poetry, he must content himself with the medieval capital astride the Seine, where the towers of Notre Dame looked across the built-up bridges and narrow gabled streets to the keep of the Louvre. In 1495, Paris was still a gothic city, untouched in character by the changes that were coming about in the South. It remained, also, the centre and fortress of the old scholasticism. From Abelard to Duns Scotus, the great names of medieval philosophy had been linked with the University of Paris, and there was to be no more acrimonious defender of the old type of theology than the Sorbonne. Erasmus must have known already that he was venturing into the territories of his enemy, when he matriculated as a student of theology and installed himself in the comfortless dormitories of Montaigu.

On the other hand, as he looked round with curiosity at the first capital city in which he had lived, he saw many things to encourage him and stimulate his interest. The city was seething with excitement about the Italian wars. The young King Charles VIII, full of romantic dreams of paladins and of recovering the kingdom of Naples, had planned an invasion of Italy which turned out to be a triumphal progress—until the very end, when he was attacked and forced to fight at Fornovo in July 1495. In the autumn, when Erasmus was just making new acquaintances in Paris, the news of the battle fired them all with pride. The serious historian, Gaguin, concluded a letter written apparently in October to his new friend the Augustinian canon, with the joyful and proud news of this victory. One of the heralds who had accompanied the army, nicknamed Gentil Garçon, lodged in the same house as Erasmus a few months later. And through the returning army filtered into France the wonder and surprise of the invaders, face to face with a different culture and a new and gracious way of living; dazzled by painting and sculpture, by Romanesque churches all green-and-gold with mosaic, and unembattled

24

houses with *loggie* giving shelter from the southern
sun, by the luxury and leisure of the small Italian
courts and the pride of the great merchant houses of
Florence and Venice. They came back laden with
booty, sometimes only half understood; a strange
mixture of junk and priceless manuscripts and statues
from the ruins of classical Italy. The greatest treasure
of all, perhaps, was John Lascaris, the Greek scholar
whom Charles VIII brought back to adorn his court.
Together with all this there ran a wave of popular
patriotism, reflected in the writings of the time;
Gaguin himself, in publishing his History of France,
was moved by it as well as by his desire to emulate the
ancients.

For in Paris, as well as a warlike popular enthusiasm roused by the Italian campaign, there was a
spirit abroad in some circles which suited Erasmus
much better—an atmosphere in which he could
breathe. When he wrote to Gaguin to introduce himself, (a too flattering letter to which we only possess
Gaguin's reply) and sent a few of his poems, he knew
that Gaguin was the most considerable figure in a
small circle of outward-looking friends, fired like
Erasmus with the love of the new learning. A few days
later, a blank page in Gaguin's *History* had to be filled
up, and somehow the printer was induced to offer it to
the young stranger. The letter of Erasmus thus
printed on the first page of the *De Origine et Gestis
Francorum Compendium* is his first published work.

For the printers were already busy in Paris and
elsewhere: Paris had been early in the field, and printing had been going on there for more than twenty
years. It is true that the records of early printing

houses show a large proportion of publications that would not interest Erasmus, especially many editions of the long prose romances of the Arthurian cycle so beloved by the later Middle Ages. But printing was becoming more common, and one of Erasmus's first ambitions was to publish his own poems and William Herman's in Paris. One slim volume, of which only two copies are now known, came out, probably in January 1496, and the *Sylva Odarum*, containing William Herman's poems and one of Erasmus's, in January 1497. Even today a young author's first printed pages seem miraculous in his eyes, but the excitement must have been intense when the volume fresh from the printer's was also one of the first printed books of all time—a record whose permanency and capacity of extension was beyond all medieval dreams.

The poems in themselves were not remarkable, and Erasmus was not proud of them in later years. They were the fruit of his youthful passion for Latin poetry, and constituted a first step into the world of literature. To have even a small volume to his name was valuable to the ambitious young man who now began to find himself a circle of literary friends. One of the closest was Fausto Andrelini, an Italian from Forlí, who had won the laurel crown for a book of love poetry in Rome, before coming to Paris in 1488. In 1496, he had attracted Charles VIII's favour with a poem on the Neapolitan campaign, and became a recognised Court poet. He lectured in the University on the classical poets, though it is said he was a perfunctory teacher, courting the applause of an ignorant audience by jests more amusing than learned. Clever, pushing, loose-principled, frivolous, he was a strange friend for the learned young monk from serious Holland. It is noticeable (if the traces that remain of Erasmus's life at this time are to be believed) that the friends Erasmus made in Paris were mainly among the foreigners who frequented that city. Gaguin indeed was French; but we find Erasmus writing to Fausto the Italian, to Christian Northoff, a young merchant of Lübeck, and to several of the young Englishmen of good family who were in Paris for their studies. Some of them were his pupils, like Thomas Grey and Robert Fisher, and the young Lord Mountjoy, who became his devoted friend.

After a year Erasmus left the College of Montaigu, of which he later gave a most uncomplimentary account in the Colloquy on Fish-eating. Hard conditions, bad sanitation, poor and inadequate food, infected water, were the lot of the students of Montaigu, and according to Erasmus the result was that some died, some contracted blindness, madness or leprosy, and many hopeful young minds were rendered unfruitful. "I know well enough," says one character in an early Colloquy, "that the louse is a scholar's companion." The régime of the College was indeed extremely severe, and may have better suited the two great men who were later to be attracted to it by its reputation for learning—Calvin and Ignatius Loyola.

Erasmus spent all the remainder of his time in Paris in lodgings of one sort or another. His letters give glimpses of his daily life, spent in hard work, for he had before him an immense programme of study, but also not without its entertainments and pleasures. Walks in the vineyards which at that time clothed the slopes outside the city; discussions with friends, shrewd observation of the people of Paris, delighted amusement at domestic upheavals like the mighty battle he witnessed between his landlady and her maid and which he relates with so much malice and gusto— thus the letters sketch the ordinary background of a student's life, often hard-pressed for money, for Erasmus's patron the Bishop was kind in his promises but not always prompt in payment. Erasmus was no ordinary student, however. Already he was well known for his learning and could have had much wider and more lucrative practice as a teacher if he had liked. But his constant desire was to cut down all other responsibilities to a minimum in order to have time to learn. Some pupils he had to have, to make ends meet at all; but the important thing was leisure for the great task he had set himself.

His position at this time was in fact ambiguous, and it needed careful manœuvring. He was, of course, an Augustinian canon on temporary leave of absence from the monastery, and the Prior if dissatisfied with him might recall him at any time. Several letters are preserved which Erasmus wrote to the Prior of Steyn, Nicholas Werner, about this time, carefully putting the best interpretation on his activities, mentioning his important friends, and giving pieces of news interesting to the Order, like the description of the great procession of January 12th, 1497. On this occasion the shrine of Ste. Geneviève was brought down from the Abbey at the top of the hill to Notre Dame at the bottom, the Abbot and Brethren of Erasmus's order escorting it barefoot, the Bishop and all the congregation coming out of the Cathedral to meet it in a

grand procession, praying for relief from the rain and
floods that had devastated the city. "Now," writes
Erasmus, "we have a quite cloudless sky." In these
letters the writer is on his best behaviour and obviously keeping on the right side of the authorities. He
represents himself as an earnest student of theology,
and certainly one of his aims was to obtain his degree
in divinity. But his real feelings on the subject of the
theological Faculty of Paris and of scholastic theology
in general, are given pungently in a letter to Thomas
Grey written later in 1497. He spins a witty tale of
Epimenides the Cretan, a classical Rip van Winkle,
whose prolonged sleep Erasmus mockingly associates
with the soporific effects of the old theological sciences, and then he bursts out into picturesque mockery.
"What if you saw Erasmus sit gaping among those
blessed Scotists, while Gryllard is lecturing from his
lofty chair? If you observed his contracted brow, his
staring eyes, his anxious face, you would say he was
another man. They assert that the mysteries of this
science cannot be comprehended by one who has any
commerce at all with the Muses or the Graces. If you
have touched good letters, you must unlearn what you
have learnt; if you have drunk of Helicon, out with
the draught again. I do my best to speak nothing in
true Latin, nothing elegant or witty, and I seem to
make some progress. There is hope that they will
acknowledge Erasmus some time or other." In other
words, this submission to a most distasteful discipline
may have the desired result—a bachelor's degree. But
in sudden seriousness he ends his letter: "Sweet Grey,
do not mistake me. I would not have you interpret
this as directed against Theology itself, which, as you

know, I have always regarded with special reverence. I have only amused myself in making game of some pseudo-theologians of our time, for nothing is more rotten than their brains, nothing more barbarous than their language, nothing duller than their interests, nothing thornier than their learning, nothing rougher than their manners, nothing more hypocritical than their lives, more venomous than their speech or blacker than their hearts. Farewell."

So much for the studies on which Erasmus was ostensibly engaged. They were the *raison d'être* of his being in the French capital at all, but his heart was certainly not in them. It was as poet and essayist that he was best known, for besides the two small publications of poetry already mentioned, he wrote several short treatises for the benefit of his pupils (notably the one *In Praise of Marriage*, for Lord Mountjoy, as to which he said later that it was merely preaching to the converted). Yet when writing to Hector Boece, future Principal of King's College, Aberdeen, a letter which he placed as preface to his first volume of poems, he protested that he could not pretend to call himself a poet; he had served the Muses devoutly as a boy, but had sought their company little since, and did not care to challenge the criticism of the learned or face the obtuseness of the uninstructed. These disclaimers are commonplace in prefaces of the time: a book was hardly decent without one. But we may surmise that Erasmus's excuses were partly sincere: he had not yet found his true vocation. He was by no means of the Fausto type; a dallying with classical studies in dilettante fashion was not sufficient for him. A deep seriousness under his sparkle and banter inclined him

30

to look for permanent values in the return to classical culture: and that religious sense which at present seemed in abeyance would have led him willingly to the study of theology, if the theology of the day had not seemed to him so repellent. His own admixture of classical learning and religious thought was yet to seek.

The one thing he was sure of at this time was his enthusiasm for the great classical inheritance. His most popular contribution to the spread and vulgarisation of the classics was ready for publication in its earliest form when he left Paris for a visit to England in 1499: it came out in 1500, a slim little volume entitled *Adagiorum Collectanea*, containing a small selection of proverbs from the ancients, with brief explanations. It was crudely printed, but it contained some of the earliest Greek printing of the Paris presses, and it was the germ of the huge work which was to issue from the Aldine press in 1508 to delight the whole sixteenth century—the *Adagiorum Chiliades*. Everyone with any interest in learning dipped into the *Adagia*; it was a storehouse of antique wisdom and later became a volume of personal essays as well.

* * *

Erasmus and the Classics

If Erasmus had not altered his viewpoint or discovered the true harmony of his life, but had remained as he seems in his Parisian letters, a pure humanist, what would have been his legacy to mankind? It would not have been inconsiderable. He would have been foremost among the ranks of those who retaught the world how to read: his editions of classical authors,

his translations from Greek into Latin, would have
been as important or gained in importance, his name
would have been that of a pioneer into the realms of
modern scholarship. Not that he always proceeded
along lines approved of today. In the words of a great
Erasmian scholar, P. S. Allen:

"It has been said of Erasmus that he propounded
the problem of scholarship, but did little to solve it;
and it must be confessed that this latter part is true
enough. But his failings were the failings of his
time—an age when archæology and palæography
were in their cradles, and textual criticism knew
only the boldest and most dashing methods. His
merit was to perceive that the invention of printing
had brought in a new era of critical study, when a
text once well and truly fashioned to embody the
sum of existing knowledge, could become a tool for
hundreds of scholars, identical and invariable, on
which each could rely, knowing that his friend was
using precisely the same; also a standard by which
new-found manuscripts could be tested. And thus
the quest of critical accuracy moved at one bound
to a higher plane. Yet not for this does the world
praise and love him today."[1]

Erasmus was not destined to remain a scholar only.
But the vision of his youth never left him, and he
continued to work on the rehabilitation of classical
literature to the end of his life. His publications include
editions of Cicero, Quintus Curtius, the *Historia
Augusta*, Horace, Livy, Ovid, Persius, Plautus, Pliny's
Natural History, Seneca's tragedies, Suetonius, Publius
Syrius, and Terence; among the Greeks, either in the

[1] *Erasmus*, a lecture, 1922.

original or in Latin versions, Æsop, Aristotle, Demosthenes, Euripides, Galen, Socrates, Josephus, Libanius, Lucian, Plutarch's minor works, Ptolemy, and Xenophon.[1] His conviction of the values and maturity of classical thought, and his aliveness to the necessity of establishing it in the purest form, contributed to inspire his whole century with the same ideals.

Much could be said, and much has indeed been said, about the key position held by Erasmus in the spread of the Revival of Learning. He was peculiarly fitted for the work of vulgarisation, being quick, enthusiastic, and occasionally somewhat slapdash— given to writing "*stans pede in uno*," as he put it. Only an astonishingly swift worker could have covered the ground as he did, constantly interrupted by illness and by the incessant journeys of which his life was full. For close on the last thirty years of that life he was generally regarded as the greatest classical scholar of his time, and that not only, one surmises, because of his untiring labours, but because of the kinship of his mind and outlook with that of the classical world. He felt more at home with antiquity than with the world into which he was born.

Two observations seem worth making here, in illustration of Erasmus's connection with his time. First, it has often been remarked that he shows no sympathy with the artistic side of the Renaissance. This is true in a narrow sense: he never seems to have had any interest in painting (except for a doubtful allusion in early youth) or in architecture, and

[1] See Preserved Smith, *Erasmus*, New York, 1923; *Bibliotheca Erasmana*, Ghent, 1893.

33

descriptions of scenery or of visual beauty are rare in his writings, though they do occur sometimes (e.g. the long letter written from Constance, which describes the beauty of the mountain scenery with such sincere delight). But the working of the æsthetic sense may often be canalised, and in Erasmus's case it all ran to a preoccupation with literary style. His extreme care for elegance of diction and the exactly right word, his essays on language, on letter-writing, his own inimitable and unmistakable turn of phrase and happy fluency, are his share in the æsthetic creativeness of the Renaissance. And as Huizinga remarks, the ebullience and richness of the Renaissance are there too. The very idea of writing a whole book on Copiousness is worthy of the period of Rabelais, and in this book (*De duplici Copia*) and in his *Colloquies* Erasmus makes it his business to increase the Latin fluency of his generation by amassing idioms, turns of phrase and richness of vocabulary—often twenty or thirty ways of saying the same thing, culled from a wide knowledge of ancient authors and collected with a loving delight in sheer variety of language. In this Erasmus is the fitting representative of the Intake aspect of the Renaissance.

Secondly, in putting within reach of his age the maturer thought and the more sensitive style of the Greek and Latin authors, Erasmus was not in the least hypnotised by their grandeur and importance. He wished to graft on to his own time the best branches from the classical tree, but a blind subservience to the writers of antiquity seemed to his common-sense mind merely the substitution of one tyranny for another. In this as in other domains Erasmus remained free. He spoke his mind on the subject towards the end of his life, in the dialogue called *Ciceronianus* (1527), which is worth reading as an open statement of the dangers attendant on the unquestioning worship of the classics which was so vital a part of the Renaissance. The dialogue, in fact, has a flavour of what was later to become known as the Quarrel of the Ancients and Moderns. It concentrates mainly on the problem of imitation—the proper attitude to adopt when faced with the overpowering influence of a culture greater than one's own.

The dialogue is as natural and racy as any Colloquy. There are three speakers: Bulephorus and his friend Hypologus see in the distance their acquaintance Nosoponus, and confer a little on his case before accosting him. Bulephorus explains that Nosoponus has fallen a victim to a severe malady, and the only way to get into touch with him is to pretend to be afflicted by it too. Up comes Nosoponus, and a few tactful questions reveal that he is pining away for love of an ideal—he longs to acquire the name of Ciceronian. Yes indeed, says Bulephorus, so do I, and how do you go about it? Nosoponus then sketches out a strict programme and his account of his life is full of comedy. He started by making a list of all the words and phrases used in the works of Cicero. No word not found in Cicero was admissible; and even another form of a word so found, a different case of a noun or part of a verb, could not be used if that particular case or inflection was not found in Cicero. He marked the authentic words of Cicero in red in his dictionary, anything else in black. To study this sacred vocabulary he shut himself up in a library like

35

a padded cell, remote from the world; kept his mind free from all other cares—needless to say, he remained a bachelor!—and refused to take up any responsibility or public position. To keep his head clear, he had only a light lunch and no dinner, and embarked on a night of study fortified only by ten currants and three coriander seeds. The propitious nights for study were chosen beforehand. (How? asks Bulephorus. Well, returns Nosoponus, I bought a book on astrology.) Each sentence of anything he writes costs him a whole night's work, and then he writes it ten times over. His Latin must be purely that of Cicero, and is therefore not suitable for everyday purposes: he uses French or Dutch (German?) for that. But he has certain set Ciceronian phrases with which to meet certain eventualities.

So far the poor crazed creature whose head has been turned by the adoration of a name. Now Bulephorus takes up the discussion and gently begins to point out that the sincerest proof of admiration is to imitate with discretion. Cicero's style was not impeccable, many of his works have perished, and how is his language to express things unknown to him, for example the range of Christian thought?

And come to that, who can be called Ciceronian? Together the friends go through a long list of names, first the Latin authors, and then the writers of the Christian era down to their own day. ("I'll suggest Erasmus Roterodamus, if you like." "What! You said you were going to speak of writers! Far from numbering him among the Ciceronians, I don't even count him as a writer at all.") Bulephorus proceeds to point out how useless such strained eloquence is, and

bought at how high a price. Nosoponus says finally:
"Well, what do you advise? Are we to throw Cicero
out and listen to him no more?" This gives Bulephorus
his chance, and the final pages of the dialogue give
Erasmus's considered opinion about this burning
question of the proper imitation of the classics: the
most important thing of all is that speech should be
the mirror of the soul. "What pleases the reader best,
is to feel that he knows the feelings, character, intellect and mind of the writer as well as if he had spent
several years in his company." Bulephorus adds—
and it is Erasmus speaking—that as a boy he liked all
poets, but as soon as he came to know Horace all the
others seemed unattractive. Why? Because there was
between them some hidden kinship of the mind, per-
ceptible even in the silent pages of a book. "I approve
of imitation, not of one chosen author from whom one
dare not stray by a line, but imitation of any trait in
any author which is excellent in itself and in harmony
with your own mind . . . so he that reads will not
recognise a thought stolen from Cicero, but see instead
the child sprung from your own brain like Pallas from
the head of Jove, its parent's living image."

In a word, it is the spirit and not the letter which is
to be imitated. The *Deffence et Illustration de la Langue
Francoyse* did not state the case more clearly.

Erasmus had a strictly common-sense outlook on
the culture which he was among the first to restore.
He knew that servile reproduction of a model serves
no purpose, and that while the ancients had so much
to give to the modern world, the Christian era had
its own treasures which were not to be found in the
storehouses of antiquity. A free choice and inter-

weaving of the best from both worlds was his hope for humanity; and though humanity has never quite risen to his expectations, that interweaving was substantially what did happen as the outcome of the Renaissance. It was his gift to see clearly what should be the role of classical culture as the formative influence of the new world. It has been suggested[1] that in their adoration of the classics, the men of the Renaissance were even more subservient to authority than the men of the Middle Ages; that the opening up of new ways was the result, not of a new spirit of independence, but of the impact of old ideas upon a different set of environmental facts. Thus it is the looking backwards which prompts the step forward, but only indirectly. In the case of Erasmus as in that of Montaigne, this is not wholly true; the adoration of the classics developed in them a native independence of mind, and their choice among classical writers betrayed their liking for direct observation and criticism (Erasmus's favourite author seems to have been Lucian, Montaigne's Plutarch). But there is a sense in which Erasmus also is an illustration of the fact that the supremacy of the ancients was only fruitful when combined with a new set of circumstances. The mental atmosphere of the classical world might appear to him as maturer than the medieval outlook, but on the spiritual side it was Christianity which possessed maturity, the precepts of Jesus being representative of an infinitely more developed moral outlook than that of the classics. To this synthesis he came round about the close of the century, and it was the continual reference to Christian standards which

[1] Butterfield, *The Statecraft of Machiavelli*, Bell, 1940.

allowed him to look with a clear selective eye on the great achievements of antiquity.

One thing he did not see; in using French or Dutch for everyday matters and keeping Latin for special occasions, the Ciceronian was right and Erasmus was wrong. He imagined that the Republic of Letters was to continue to use Latin as its *lingua franca*, purified and ennobled by contact with the classics. It was much more use to him than the dialect to which he had been born. His own Latin style, with its charm and wit and elasticity, was equal to as many occasions as any modern language could have been. But that was rare; and when Bulephorus complained that Ciceronian Latin could never hope to express the modern world, he would only have needed to go a step farther to meet the truth of the future—the slow abandonment of an ancient and common tongue.

Chapter *Two*

The Philosophy of Christ

IN the summer of 1499, Erasmus paid his first visit
to England. It was to be a short holiday, which
events prolonged to a period of six months, and yet
it seems to have been, psychologically, one of the
turning-points of his development. To England and
to the new English friends falls the honour of resolving
his inner conflict, or rather of bringing into harmony
interests which had hitherto existed side by side without apparent connection. In these six months he
caught the first true glimpse of the purpose and the
meaning of his life.

Erasmus came to England as the guest of the young
Lord Mountjoy, and for the first time he found himself treated as an equal by the great, staying in aristo-
cratic houses, catching courtly ways, hunting, and
enjoying the blandishments of the ladies. His first
extant letter from England is almost too well known
to quote, but it expresses better than anything else
his naïve pleasure :[1]

"We too have made progress in England. The
Erasmus you once knew is now become almost a
sportsman, no bad rider, a courtier of some practice,
bows with politeness, smiles with grace, and all this
in spite of himself. If you too are wise, you too will
fly over here . . . To take one attraction out of many :

[1] *The Epistles of Erasmus*, tr. Nichols, I, p. 213.

there are nymphs here with divine features, so
gentle and kind that you may well prefer them to
your Camenae. Besides, there is a fashion which
cannot be commended enough. Wherever you go,
you are received on all hands with kisses; when you
take leave, you are dismissed with kisses. If you go
back, your salutes are returned to you. When a
visit is paid, the first act of hospitality is a kiss, and
where guests depart, the same entertainment is
repeated; wherever a meeting takes place there is
kissing in abundance, in fact, whatever way you
turn, you are never without it. Oh Faustus, if you
had once tasted how sweet and fragrant these
kisses are, you would indeed wish to be a traveller,
not for ten years, like Solon, but for your whole
life, in England."

He was taken about by his new friends, notably
on the excursion to Eltham Palace, where he was
presented to the group of Henry VII's children, with
the exception of Arthur, Prince of Wales. The precocious boy of eight who was to be Henry VIII
impressed him by his royal bearing, and embarrassed
him by sending him a note during dinner asking for
something from his pen. The poem on England which
resulted was written in three days, with much toil,
says Erasmus, for it was so many years since he had
written verse: and yet often during his English stay
he describes himself as a poet. Not only when writing
to the irrepressible Faustus, but to such serious new
friends as John Colet, now lecturing at Oxford and
later to be Dean of St. Paul's, he ends a grave letter[1]
on a subject of Biblical interpretation: "You see, my

[1] Allen, I, 109.

dear Colet, how I observe decorum by ending so theological a discussion with the fables of the poet. But as Horace says, you may drive out nature with a pitchfork and she will surely return." He went to Oxford, and one of the most charming of his English letters describes a dinner party, at which Colet was the host, and Richard Charnock, the prior of St. Mary's College where Erasmus was staying, Erasmus himself and several others were guests. Delighted with his evening, Erasmus enumerates to John Sixtin, who was also invited but absent, the roll of the guests, adding that he himself was there "lest a poet should be wanting to the banquet." The talk fell on the subject of Cain, and why his sacrifice should have been less pleasing to God than Abel's. Colet produced the original theory that it was because in tilling the soil Cain had shown less faith in the goodness of the Creator, and more confidence in his own efforts, than the guileless Abel who sacrificed the best lamb of his flock. Argument grew heated, and Erasmus decided, as became a poet, to introduce a lighter note: and there is a pleasant art of story-telling in his frivolous tale of Cain's real delinquency, which was (according to him) the preposterous impertinence of bribing the angel at the gates of Eden to give him some of the seed—so much finer than mere earthly grain—of the garden which men had forfeited by their disobedience.

The group of English humanists were surprised and delighted with the wit and vivacity of the young Augustinian canon. He, on his part, fell in love with the whole atmosphere, and made friends for life with those men whose names still bear a gentle sweetness,

Colet, Grocyn, Linacre, More. Perhaps for the first time he met with the best elements of an educated society. In Paris his friends were not scholars of the first rank; he does not seem at this time to have been personally introduced to Lefèvre d'Etaples. Furthermore, in Paris there was the shadow of the Sorbonne. By his attachment to the humanities, Erasmus was wronging theology, he was ranging himself with the suspect, stealing time from his avowed occupations to spend it on poetry and the mere art of writing. But in England he was free from any such disapproval. The breath of Italy had blown stronger there and had met no such chilling opposition.

Erasmus's new friends were charmed with his learning, his ease, his human common sense and his laughter, and some of them, above all Colet, perceived beneath it all qualities that Erasmus himself did not quite know he possessed. There is a letter of Erasmus to Colet which is plainly the echo of a crucial conversation between the two friends. Erasmus expresses his interest in the lectures on the Epistles of Paul by which Colet, so young and as yet without a doctor's degree, is attracting great audiences in the University of Oxford. To the suggestion that he, Erasmus, should attempt to interpret in the same way another part of the Scriptures, possibly of the Old Testament, Erasmus answers a decided negative. He has often, during his lifetime and afterwards, been accused of intellectual arrogance, but this letter is a deeply sincere expression of humility. The despiser of the Schoolmen has met the Theology of his own heart at last, and he knows that he has not yet the necessary grasp of experience to take on such a task, nor the confidence to face an audience with such a matter in hand. "How could I teach what I have never learnt?" he asks, and the question lets in a flood of light. Erasmus had seen in Colet's approach to the Scriptures the vision of a new world, in which Theology was to be no longer a matter of convention, or of argument and proof on subjects divorced from the everyday life of man, but the direct interpretation, in the light of common sense and widely-culled learning, of the documents of the Faith themselves. Here at last the wandering pieces of the puzzle fell into place; Erasmus the enthusiastic humanist and Erasmus the unwilling student of Theology coalesced into one person, the man whose life-work was to be the furthering of one great cause—the setting of the wisdom of the ancients at the service of the interpretation of Christianity and the betterment of man.

It is noticeable that the discussions Erasmus reports between himself and Colet are on the psychological interpretation of the Bible. They discussed at length the meaning of Christ's agony in the garden; was the human nature of Jesus open to the experience of human fear, or was there, as Colet suggested, some other secret in that spiritual conflict? It was not now a matter of discussing abstract propositions or traditional aspects of theology. The ideas which had been forming in Erasmus's mind for many years, encouraged by his reading of Valla and the early Fathers, but kept secret because they were frowned upon by the authorities which ruled his life—these ideas crystallised out during his conversations with Colet, and he saw before him a vista of work and achievement, the goal of it all being the modern

44

interpretation of the Bible. During the years which followed his first English summer, years of hard work, continual restless movement from one place to another, and desperate money-grubbing, Erasmus kept his goal well in sight. It was the star of his life, and under its leadership he struggled with Greek, begged and scrounged for subsistence and leisure, and began to write on the Epistles of St. Paul, keeping his work well in the dark until he should know enough Greek to satisfy his own standards of accuracy.

He went back to Paris at the end of the summer, and from then until 1506 he oscillated between Paris and the Low Countries, spending some time at Tournehem in Hainaut, the residence of Batt's patroness, the lady of Veere. The lack of any stable source of income at all made this the most sordid period of Erasmus's life. The situation was not helped by the severe application of a law of Henry VII forbidding the export of any coin from English ports, with the result that Erasmus, misinformed on the point, found himself mulcted of all but £2 out of the £20 in his possession at the custom-house at Dover. He was bitterly indignant, and never forgot the injury. It meant returning at once to the hand-to-mouth existence of his Paris days, and his letters to the faithful friend Batt, who was attempting to squeeze funds for Erasmus from his patroness, take on an acrimonious tone. Yet he never wavered from his purpose, which was now to perfect his Greek. "You may ask why I am so pleased with the example of Cato the Censor, as to be learning Greek at my age. I answer, Reverend Father, that if I had had this mind when a boy, or rather if the times had been more favourable to me, I should have been the happiest man in the world. As it is, I am determined that it is better to learn late than to be without that knowledge which it is of the utmost importance to possess. We had a taste of this learning a long time ago, but it was only with the tip of the tongue, as they say; and having lately dipped deeper into it, we see, what we have often read in the most weighty authors, that Latin erudition, however ample, is crippled and imperfect without Greek. We have in Latin at best some small streams and turbid pools, while they have the clearest springs and rivers flowing with gold." Especially is it necessary for the study of Theology. "If there is any fresh Greek to be had, I had rather pawn my coat than not get it, especially if it is something Christian, as the Psalms in Greek or the Gospels." And it was at this time that Erasmus wrote the book which first of all showed his quality and revealed some of his dearest wishes to the world.

* * *

The Enchiridion Militis Christiani

No good English title has yet been found for the *Enchiridion Militis Christiani*.[1] The word Enchiridion meaning something carried in the hand, and applying equally well to a manual or a dagger, it was translated early in England under the title "The Handsome Weapon of a Christian Knight." One cannot help regretting that this little book was not first written in a modern European language; it might

[1] Written at St. Omer in 1501, but not published till February 1503; see Allen, I, p. 229.

have ranked beside the early masterpieces of the Renaissance.

And yet Erasmus, who was apparently not so ignorant of any vernacular as has sometimes been supposed, had his public well in mind when he embarked upon his long career of popular writing in Latin. In his view the freemasonry of Latin as a common European tongue was to be not only preserved, but extended and purified by the efforts of such people as himself, so that the growing literate class should have a modern literature, not now in dog-Latin but in an easy fluent style approaching that of Rome; and yet, as we have seen, it was not to be so learned and so purist as to fail to keep up with the requirements of a new age. Erasmus made a bid for a common European tongue at a time when the thought of Europe was already beginning to run over into the many channels of the modern European languages; and from our point of view his bid may be said to have failed. But two facts remain true: that science and philosophy hesitated to abandon Latin for many generations after Erasmus's day; and that in the popular vein, no one came anywhere near Erasmus's success in using Latin as a living language, supple, clear, vivacious, saucy, and bearing the stamp of a trick of style which is all its own.

The *Enchiridion* was not published at once, and did not at first attract much attention, but after its reprinting in 1518 it became one of the popular books of Europe, and was translated into many languages.[1] It was the first announcement of a message

[1] The English translation, published in 1534 by Wynkyn de Worde, is used here in modern form with some small alterations.

which was to run through many books and be couched in different styles, and to which Erasmus was to remain absolutely constant throughout his life. For that reason it is worth pausing over, and indeed in some ways it is the best enunciation of his message; Erasmus said it more arrestingly in other places, but he never said it better.

The *Enchiridion* differs from Erasmus's other famous popular books in being consistently serious. It may have a pungent turn of phrase here and there, but it is without the satire and banter which made the fortune of the *Colloquies* and *The Praise of Folly*. It is a plain statement of what Erasmus took the Christian life to be, a war of the spirit in which the chief weapons to use are knowledge and prayer. He sketches the conditions of the war, the goal of victory and the results of defeat, and ends by giving some practical recommendations as to the way to deal with certain temptations and conditions of mind. The fact that these terminate the book provides a sort of anti-climax, not unintentional perhaps: they accentuate the practical tone of the whole work and end it on a very modest note. It was indeed a working set of rules, written for people grappling with real difficulties of everyday life, and only suggesting here and there the mystical approach to truth which lies behind. Now and then we get glimpses of a serene beauty behind and above the struggle.

Knowledge and prayer: in the second chapter dealing with these two weapons of the spirit, Erasmus has fused together his own aspirations and the old teaching of his masters the Brethren—or so one fancies as one reads. The first thing which would strike a contemporary reader is the place accorded to secular learning in the training of the Christian mind. Here Erasmus states his position very clearly and carefully. He is ready to recommend the study of the classics, of poetry and philosophy, especially of Plato, because "those sciences fashion and quicken a child's mind"; they are the ABC of wisdom, they can teach one many things. Far be it from him to deny to pagan poetry the gift of expressing some of the works of God. But he is no longer the blind enthusiast for classical learning, and from this point he marks clearly his separation (and with him, the separation of the whole Northern Renaissance) from the neo-paganism of some Italians. These studies are a means to an end, and they are justified as a prelude to the highest study of which man's mind is capable, the study of Scripture. If one were to linger over them and grow old in them, one would be like the ancient victims of the Sirens, lost on the rocks, with one's journey stayed for ever. (Erasmus failed to take his own advice: he went on editing the classics to the end of his life.) But it will be all profit if it is done in youth, with due selection and discrimination, and "after the manner of a man that intendeth but to pass over the country only and not to dwell or inhabit"—and above all, "if everything be applied and referred to Christ."

It is the second part of the chapter which recalls the teaching of the Brethren, for in it Erasmus shows how far he was from pure rationalism. He is describing the approach to the Scriptures, which must be made with a mind sharpened by culture, but also with a heart purified by reverence, and able to go beneath the surface and understand the inner meaning of the word. For the letter killeth but the spirit giveth life.

The high point of the *Enchiridion* is reached in an expansion of this subject which occupies the whole of Chapter XIII. This would be the second point especially noticed by any contemporary reader. It is an eloquent and impassioned plea for a return to the realisation of the inwardness of the spiritual life. In a world where religion had largely become a matter of ceremonies and conventional observances, Erasmus, the pupil of the Brethren, uses the reserves of his eloquence to make a fervent restatement of the essential character of religion, the cult of the invisible. The opening of the chapter is Platonic, seeing in the visible world elements which are symbolic of the features of the invisible world, earthly beauty as a reflection of the beauty of the soul. Between the two worlds stands man, belonging in part to each, and his journey is from one to the other. Everything partakes of the two natures: "the gospel hath her flesh, she hath also her spirit"; and it is the spirit only which profits a man. "God is a mind," Erasmus says characteristically: *Mens est*, and with the mind He must be served. Erasmus has much to say on the outward manifestations of religion, the saying of mass, going in pilgrimage, reverencing of relics; they are of small value compared to the spiritual things. "Honourest thou the bones of Paul hid in the shrine, and honourest thou a piece of his carcase shining through a glass, and regardest not thou the whole mind of Paul shining through his letters?" The very apostles themselves, privileged as they were in the physical presence of Christ, remained weak and childish and uncomprehending until His bodily presence was replaced by the Spirit in their hearts. "The corporal presence of Christ is unprofitable unto health. And dare we in any corporal thing beside that put perfect piety, that is to say, the love and honour of God?"

This was a bold statement in the year 1501, and Erasmus knew it would wake much opposition; it launches him into the first of many challenges against "certain preachers which with right good will sing these things, inwardly in their own stomachs looking verily not unto Christ, but unto their own advantage, through whose either superstition without learning, or feigned holiness, I am compelled oftentimes to shew and declare that I in no wise rebuke or check the corporal ceremonies of Christian men and devout minds of simple persons . . . And because they are somewhat necessary to young infants in Christ, till they wax older and grow up unto a perfect man: therefore it is not meet they should be disdained of them which are perfect, lest by their example the weak person should take harm . . . But to worship Christ with visible things instead of invisible, and in them to put the highest point of religion, and from them to stand in thine own conceit, to condemn other men, to set thy whole mind upon them, and also to die in them . . . this is verily to depart from the law of the gospel which is spiritual, and fall into certain superstition of ceremonies like unto the Jews." The trouble is increased by the fact that this ritualistic view of religion is held not only by the ignorant and simple, but by the very priesthood which should be pointing the way to the spiritual life. Erasmus becomes very explicit: "It is no great thing to have trodden the steps of Christ with thy bodily heels, but it is a great thing to follow the steps of Christ in affection. If it be a very great thing to have touched the sepulchre of Christ, shall it not be also a very great thing to have expressed the mystery of his burying? Thou accusest and utterest thy sins to a priest, which is a man: take heed how thou accusest and utterest them before God, for to accuse them afore him is to hate them inwardly. Thou believest perchance all thy sins and offences to be washed away at once with a little paper or parchment sealed with wax, with a little money or images of wax offered, with a little pilgrimage going. Thou art utterly deceived and clean out of the way!" This, sixteen years before the revolt of Luther.

The chapter ends with a serene and robust picture of the true believer, "excellent in Christ, large in charity, strong and stable both in prosperity and adversity, looking beside small things and enforcing up to things of most profit, full of mirth, full also of knowledge, which knowledge whosoever refuseth, them doth that noble lord of all knowledge refuse." It is a definition (before the name) of the *Philosophia Christi*, strangely like Montaigne's rapturous definition of Philosophy, smiling and accessible, approached by *"routes doux-fleurantes"*. And finally Erasmus's matter-of-fact pen approaches an unusually spiritual eloquence: "Lift up thyself as it were with certain steps of the ladder of Jacob, from the body to the spirit, from the visible world to the invisible, from the letter to the mystery, from things of the senses to

52

things of the mind, from things gross and compound to things single and pure. Whosoever after this manner shall approach and draw near to the Lord, the Lord of his part shall again approach and draw nigh to him. And if thou for thy part shalt endeavour to arise out of the darkness and troubles of the sensual powers, he will come towards thee pleasantly and for thy profit, out of this light inaccessible, and out of that silence unthinkable, in which not only all tumult of the senses, but also all imaginations of the intelligence do cease and keep silence."

So Erasmus begins in the *Enchiridion* his work of liberation. It stated all his future policy: his vision of the classical world as preparing the mind for the revelation of God, his vision of a practical Christianity based on knowledge of the Gospel and the spiritual understanding of a purified heart, his denunciation of the worldly and profiteering elements in the religious organisations of his day, especially of the monastic orders, his conviction that religion is an attitude of mind and an ethical code based on reverence of a Person, his insistence on the practical outcome of all belief. Through the whole book runs his persistent effort not only to think clearly and express himself simply, but to bring his reader face to face with fact, to get behind all accepted ideas and all respect of persons, to think reality. This effort to see the world anew was the mark of his maturity and the basis of his influence over Europe.

* * *

The concluding words of the *Enchiridion* contained a promise. Speaking of the value of St. Paul's letters,

and recommending a constant reading of them (in
the words of Horace, later to be taken up by Du Bellay,
"Feuillette de main nocturne et journelle ces vielz
exemplaires") Erasmus says that he has begun a
commentary on the Epistles, and intends to show that
he has followed the study of classical literature from
his youth for a high purpose—not for pride or empty
and selfish pleasure, but to adorn with it the temple
of God. This is the first mention of his work on the
New Testament which was to culminate in the publication of the Greek text in 1516. We find traces of it at
intervals in his letters: writing to Colet in 1504 he
says he has written four volumes of his study on the
Epistle to the Romans, but is held up by his lack of
Greek, which he has been working at for three years;
his knowledge is still insufficient. In 1506, writing
from London, he dedicated to the Archbishop of
Canterbury, William Warham, a translation into
Latin of two plays of Euripides, *Hecuba* and *Iphigenia
in Aulis*. In the preface he explains that he has undertaken this translation as a first venture, to try his hand
on something difficult, but belonging to profane literature, as a preparation to translating the text of
Scripture. At least, he thought, if mistakes crept in,
they would not be insults to Holy Writ. Here Erasmus
is putting into action his own precepts: he has a sincere admiration for Euripides, as the estimate of his
style in this preface shows, but for all their beauty the
works of the poet are to be part of the schooling which
leads to the highest goal of wisdom—understanding
of the words of Christ. The greater work had in fact
begun to take shape; he apparently left behind him
in England a draft of his Latin translation of the New

54

Testament, which Colet caused to be copied between 1506 and 1509[1].

This second stay in England renewed Erasmus's acquaintance with the London circle of men of letters, those whom he describes, in a letter to his monastery in Holland, as "five or six Latin and Greek scholars of deepest learning, such as not even Italy herself could now show." Yet Italy remained an unvisited paradise, and when in 1506, the opportunity arose to make the long-postponed journey to Italy in the company of the young sons of Henry VIII's doctor, Erasmus took it with alacrity. He left London with the boys and their tutor about the beginning of June, delayed a while in Paris, but was in Italy by the autumn; and on September 5th, 1506 he took his doctor's degree at the University of Turin.

As he made the long and slow journey across the Alps, he wrote a poem on the inconvenience of old age, which may seem to us premature, since he was barely forty; but in the sixteenth century forty was well past the prime of life, and Montaigne could say at thirty-eight that he had already lived much longer than the generality of mankind. Erasmus's poem—it was almost his last—is a farewell to levity and a dedication of his remaining years to the service of Christ alone. There is a wistful charm about the backward look over the years of his youth, recalling his childish games, his ardour for learning as a boy, the quarrels of the doctors from which he turned with passion to the fair visions of the poets, the fervour of activity

[1] This manuscript exists in three parts, two at the British Museum and one at the University Library of Cambridge. See Allen, II, 384 introd.

which has led him through secular and sacred studies to the threshold of old age. What there is left of life may be the shorter and the less valuable part, but that at least shall be consecrated to Christ. Farewell then, not only to the trifles of youth, pleasures, jests and laughter, but also to syllogisms and versifying. The serious work of life lies ahead.

This is not to say that in Italy Erasmus would devote himself to Theology. Quite the contrary: getting his doctor's degree in divinity at the earliest possible moment, he devoted the rest of his time to humanistic studies, for Italy was their home. He had now a clear conception of what he was working for, and the gap to be filled was still in the fuller knowledge of Greek. He went with his pupils first to Bologna, but the country was in the grip of war, and the party soon found it advisable to move to Florence, where they arrived in October 1506. It is curious that of all Erasmus's Italian experiences the stay in Florence appears to have left the least impression: and that was in 1506, when Leonardo, Michael Angelo, Raphael, fra Bartolommeo, and Andrea del Sarto were all at work! Erasmus wanted not painting, but Greek. He spent his time in Florence translating Lucian and grumbling because war prevented him from pursuing his humanistic studies: and as de Nolhac says, he did not even know that the name of the secretary of the Republic was Machiavelli.

Back in Bologna in November, he witnessed a triumphal entry of the Pope, Julius II, who was seeking to reclaim from his enemies some of the territories of the Papacy. After regaining Bologna from the Bentevogli, the Pope ("a true Julius," said

Erasmus) rode in through a breach in the city wall, and through decorated streets and arches of greenery, preceded by a hundred young noblemen symbolising the subdued population of Romagna as in a Roman triumph. Erasmus watched, no doubt from one of the arcades, and compared this warrior Pope, riding in such state behind the Holy Sacrament, with the very different triumphs of the Apostles. Erasmus had come to Italy with an observant and critical eye.

The story of Erasmus's stay in Italy has been told by Pierre de Nolhac in a charming and scholarly little volume, *Erasme en Italie*. We need consider here only the highlights of that journey, the culmination of so many plans and hopes. Erasmus spent most of 1507 in Bologna, remaining faithful at some cost to himself to the pact which bound him to the Boerio boys as the supervisor of their studies. He disliked their tutor, an Englishman named Clifton, and finally separated from them to go to Venice. In October 1507 he had written to Aldus Manutius, the great Venetian printer, offering him the two translated plays of Euripides, which Aldus printed together with two poems by Erasmus, in a beautiful little volume very suited to its purpose (to be presented as a New Year's gift to the author's friends). The connection with Aldus once established, a much greater project was on foot: the printing of a much extended edition of the *Adages*. For the purpose of completing this, while Aldus began the printing, Erasmus moved to Venice, and lodged with Aldus in the house of his father-in-law, Andrea da Asola, near the Rialto. Later on there was some acrimonious writing on the subject of this household, a large one of some thirty people; Erasmus represented it as conducted with too much parsimony, while his enemy Scaliger accused him of behaving there as an intemperate man and a glutton. The truth probably was that Erasmus, used to the heavier eating of the North, felt undernourished in Venice, and it is certain that the attacks of the stone to which he became subject began there. However, he had only to ask leave to make his meals in his own room, as he did, for these difficulties to cease. Aldus's circle was quite an Academy, and Greek might be spoken at table, and literary conversations go on well into the night. Everyone was interested in the *Adages*; manuscripts were lent from all sides, and help received, Erasmus says, even from people he did not know either by sight or by name. The book which resulted from these enthusiastic labours was one of the most considerable works of the Renaissance.

Outside Aldus's printing-house, the colour and light of Venice was translating itself into art. The Venetian school of painting was touching the highest point of its glory, with the two Bellini, Cima, Carpaccio, Giorgione, Palma Vecchio, Titian. One wonders whether Erasmus took much heed of the beauty of Venice or of its art, whether his eye was caught as he crossed the Rialto by the clear light on the palace façades or the reflections in the water. No doubt he was more intent on the revival of the past, on the success of the *Adages* and on the many friendships he was to take away with him from Venice.

The next place in which he stayed for any length of time was Padua, where he went to join the household of another noble pupil, Alexander Stuart, a natural son of James IV of Scotland. This young man

58

of eighteen was already Archbishop of St. Andrews, and seems to have been a remarkable youth. Erasmus was very fond of him, and drew an affectionate portrait of him in a later edition of the *Adages*, describing his handsome presence, his love of learning, the discussions on serious subjects at his table, the music and singing after dinner, the tact with which he managed his numerous household. All these things give point to the Adage against war, *Dulce bellum inexpertis*, for the young man fell by the side of his father at Flodden.

Erasmus found Padua an attractive place, more Christian than the rest of Italy, and favourable to his humanistic studies also. But war was still raging through the Peninsula, and in December 1508 the formation of the League of Cambrai, uniting the Emperor, the King of France, the King of Spain and the Pope against Venice, made it discreet to leave the territories of the Republic. Erasmus's party arrived at Siena, where the young archbishop continued his studies in law, and they all witnessed the curious games and bull-fights of Carnival time. But Erasmus was impatient now to get to the central point of his journey, and early in 1509 he took leave of the archbishop and went on alone to Rome.

Erasmus's three visits to Rome introduced him to a most cultivated circle. He was already well known, and the friends he had made elsewhere lost no time in putting him in contact with all the literary lights ·of Rome. One of the most interesting to Erasmus was Inghirami, the Pope's librarian, who may have taken him to watch Raphael beginning his paintings in the Vatican. The libraries of Rome offered him a wealth

59

of manuscripts which he never forgot, and the cardinals a welcome with which he was sincerely pleased. He looked on with curiosity and astonishment at the jests, amusements and bull-fights, and turned on the crowd of hangers-on round the Curia the same ironic glance as Du Bellay fifty years later. The paganism of some learned men and Renaissance prelates exercised his irony long after in the *Ciceronianus*; possibly his insight into the lack of sincere religion in Rome might have had a devastating effect on his point of view, if his knowledge of what was to be his life-work had not already been so clear. For him the riches of the past of Rome only reached their true value in elucidating the words of the Galilean.

The visits to Rome were in every sense a culmination of Erasmus's stay in Italy. He returned there after Alexander had gone home to Scotland, and had such a welcome from his friends that he might easily have stayed on there indefinitely, if he had cared to accept a position at the Papal court. But as usual he shied away from any proposition which might in the least endanger his freedom of mind and speech. A less dangerous prospect opened in England: an old acquaintance had just come to the throne as Henry VIII, and Erasmus's friends there wrote to him that they saw opening before them the age of gold. He decided to join Mountjoy and Colet and More, and left Italy for England in the early summer of 1509.

* * *

Erasmus was now forty, possibly a little more. His contemporaries may well have thought him at the apex of his development and success. The *Adages* had crowned his reputation for scholarship, and given him a solid basis for European fame. He was not only a Doctor at last, but he had been welcomed and fêted in the very heart of the fastnesses of humanism; the Italians had had to admit that one of the barbarians had attained the height of classical culture. What Erasmus gained from his Italian journey was not so much knowledge as confidence. He probably took almost as much Greek to Italy as he brought out of it, but he went there still diffident and seeking encouragement, and came back conscious of his power over his own time. He had been received by the most cultivated society in the world as one of themselves, and the impression this made upon his mind can be seen by the way he describes, over twenty years later, the visit he paid to Cardinal Grimani. To bear a name which acted as "open sesame" to the doors of the great: to be welcomed with deference into discussions on literature, to be advised not to leave Rome, invited to share a Cardinal's house, begged to believe his expressions of goodwill—this was a measure of the advance that had been made, since the patronage of the Bishop of Cambrai opened the doors of Steyn to a restless monk.

The increase of self-confidence was marked, and it had two plain results. In the first place, the security it gave let loose Erasmus's natural irony. He had always loved Lucian and satire, and had a pretty wit of his own, but had never indulged it much in his writings so far. The Roman scene has often seemed to increase a bent for satire, whether because of the Roman's own love for lampoons (Erasmus was greatly interested in the survival of the Pasquinades) or because the crowded stage of Roman life naturally invites the criticism of a satirical eye, as Du Bellay was soon to find. The first result in Erasmus's case is the magisterial irony of *The Praise of Folly*, with its sense of looking out over the world from a peak of wisdom, its free and bold expression of opinion gaily and subtly expressed. And other books were to follow.

Secondly, Erasmus was confirmed in his mind as to his own special mission. De Nolhac expresses a regret that he did not accept so many offers and remain in Italy. But surely Erasmus knew his business best. He knew that he was not at the summit of his work, but at the end of a long apprenticeship, that his finest achievements were still to come, and that an Erasmus attached to the Papal court would have the greatest difficulty in attaining them. That Erasmus would have been another person, not the one we know—the apostle of the northern Renaissance, the free, independent, solitary scholar, the bold exegetist and searcher of the Scriptures. The immersion in the atmosphere of Italian humanism was invaluable to him; it crowned his efforts and completed his intellectual formation; it was both a lesson and a holiday of the mind. But there was a phrase that was often under Erasmus's pen and probably on his lips, when he thought of the temptations offered by pure scholarship: it was "to grow old on the rocks of the Sirens." Learning for learning's sake was not enough. The brilliant pleasures of the Renaissance in Rome were empty toys, unless all this learning were to be only a prelude or a ladder to the achieving of the good life, all this knowledge of the intricacies of language to be a searchlight directed on to the text of Scripture. Erasmus left Rome to embark upon his true work, quietly certain where his own destiny lay.

He was not averse either to the prospect of worldly advantage held out to him by Mountjoy—"mountains of gold," as he later expressed it. And after all, where had he better friends than in England? As he rode across the mountains on his way through Europe, he was in a cheerful mood, not this time composing serious Latin verses on old age, but meditating ironically on the world as he knew it, on what he had seen in Rome. And though he weighed the folly of the world in his serious Dutch scales and found it lighter than a feather, the book which emerged from these reflections was tinged with the caustic Roman spirit, bolder and freer than anything he had written before. It was when he arrived at More's house in Bucklersbury, tired after the long journey and suffering from lumbago, with nothing to do but wait for his case of books to arrive, that he amused himself by dashing off a brilliant sketch which he called *The Praise of Folly*. It took a week—a week out of his laborious life of scholarship—and he was more than half ashamed of spending so much time on it. In the preface finally addressed to More he apologised for such triviality: but after all, serious people are not criticised for playing bowls, he pleaded, so why should scholarship not have its entertainments too? When he thought of publishing it he did not send it openly to any of his usual printers, but took it to Paris and slipped it to a friend who had it printed by a little-known French printer, Gilles Gourmont (1511). However, it was no use trying to hide *The Praise of Folly*. It delighted the

whole of Europe. Edition followed edition and translation followed translation, and like Lewis Carroll,
Erasmus was speedily more famous for the pastime of
a few idle days than for all the serious work of his life.

Besides its entertaining character, Erasmus had
other reasons for half disowning *The Praise of Folly*. It
contained a biting denunciation of the weaknesses of
the Church of Rome. Not content with exposing the
vices of princes and cardinals, the lashing tongue of
Folly held up to ridicule the Popes themselves, their
riches, their power, their worldly glory, their fierceness in threatening or excommunicating those who
rob them of Peter's pence, and above all, their fond-
ness for war. The fact that Erasmus dared to contrast
all this with the simplicity and long-sufferingness of
the Apostles is the clearest demonstration of his
reasons for leaving Rome. No such freedom would
have been possible under the shadow of St. Peter's
and if Erasmus desired anything passionately during
his whole life, it was freedom. He never returned to
Rome.

And yet how he longed for it! It may be said at once
that the visit to England was largely a disillusionment.
It had its pleasant sides: he met his old friends, More
and Grocyn, who both at different times gave him
hospitality, Colet, as devoted as ever, Archbishop
Warham, uniformly warmhearted and generous of
money and encouragement, Linacre, and Fisher, the
Bishop of Rochester, who was Chancellor of the
University of Cambridge and a former Fellow of
Queens'. It was through his invitation that Erasmus
was invited to leave London and take up residence at
Cambridge to lecture in Greek. Erasmus had hoped

for royal patronage rather than for academic employment, but as the former seemed slow in coming he accepted the latter. He left London for Cambridge in the late summer of 1511, just after a bout of what was then called sweating sickness. The journey by horseback took two days, the horse went lame and fell three times on his nose, the rain streamed down and finally thunder and lightning ushered them into Cambridge. Erasmus sat in his rooms in Queens' in a bad temper: he still felt ill, the Cambridge beer was execrable and there was no wine to be had, and could his new friend Ammonius, to whom he was writing, send him a cask of Greek wine, not too sweet?

Erasmus did not get on well with universities. This was to be expected, for they tended to be conservative and were the last citadels of the old learning, while the new lines of thought and humanistic appreciation were suspect to them. So, to the die-hards, was the study of Greek, and it was a sign of enlightenment that Cambridge should arrange lectures in Greek even by the foremost scholar in Europe. But there is little evidence of their being largely attended, and Erasmus speaks grudgingly of his academic work, as if his audiences were small. Scotists and Thomists there were in abundance, and he finds himself defending Colet from their attacks. He intended to return almost at once to London, where all his enlightened friends were, but for one reason and another he spent in all nearly two and a half years in Cambridge. His letters to Ammonius, who was an Italian from Lucca now acting as Latin secretary to the King, are full of complaints. Ammonius sends him wine, but the Cambridge carriers are dishonest and extortionate, and the cask arrives half empty and he has to pay sixpence on it. He and Ammonius agree that there are grave faults in the common people of England—they are neither civil nor clean. Erasmus also finds the University people both dull and self-conceited; he calls them in his humanistic terms of abuse "Cyprian bulls and dung-eaters," who think moreover that they are the only people who feed on ambrosia and Jupiter's brain! And when he wants things transcribed, what a University! "No one is to be found at any price, who can write even tolerably." He is ill, too, with a complaint not quite new to him, the stone. Perhaps it is due to that Cambridge beer? At all events he had two attacks of it during the time he spent there. His restless mind was for ever turning over new plans of trying his fortune somewhere else.

And yet there were moments when he was reconciled to life at Cambridge. It is true he would rather spend summer than winter there, and proposes to go back to London in January so that he and Ammonius can keep each other warm (any kind of room will do, if it has a fire and no draughts). "This place does not displease me altogether," he writes cautiously, "and I can see that there is something to be earned if one will be a man of all work." In point of fact the University appealed in 1512 to Lord Mountjoy to assist them in paying the "immensium stipendium" which they had promised to their Greek professor, who could only be induced to remain by ready payment. Erasmus lectured not only on Greek grammar but on St. Jerome, and in the quiet of Cambridge he worked enthusiastically on his dual objective, classical texts and the early documents of Christianity. Tradition sees him as pacing the riverside walk opposite the old red-brick front of Queens', and it is said that when Ascham went to Cambridge in 1530, he heard from Garrett the bookseller (with whom Erasmus had probably lodged) how the great scholar "when he had been sore at his boke, for lack of better exercise would take his horse and ryde about the Markette Hill and come agayne." Some of the Cambridge colleges already wore an old and settled look, in Erasmus's time: Peterhouse, Clare, Pembroke, Corpus Christi. The colleges of the Renaissance were still to be built, but not far from Queens', along the banks of the meandering streams that flowed through the place called Little Bridges, was the mighty chapel of King's, which had been building for over sixty years, and now stood alone in the midst of the vast empty space which had been cleared for it. The actual fabric of the chapel was completed in 1515, and Erasmus may well, on his after-dinner walks, have watched the masons putting the final touches to the intricate stonework. There is no evidence of his views about that, but his reflections on visiting the shrine of St. Thomas of Canterbury, probably in 1512, were amply recorded in a famous Colloquy: and he may possibly have looked quizzically at King's also.

The main difficulty about life in Cambridge was the prevalence of the plague. True, it was even worse in London, and that was one reason why Erasmus preferred to spend the summer in Cambridge: but in 1513, the pestilence was so bad that the University was emptied. Erasmus took refuge occasionally at the village of Landbeach, five miles out, where his friend William Gunnell lived with his parents and kept a

67

school. He also kept Erasmus's horse, and there are many letters relating to the care of this animal, with affectionate messages to the Gunnell family, as if a week-end in the country, in this little thatched village with its plain old church, had been one of the humanist's consolations during this time. But in the country there was one drawback—wine was unobtainable! So, if one had to choose between risking the plague and having no wine, it was clear that the plague was the lesser evil. Erasmus spent nearly all that stricken summer in Cambridge, waiting to be paid thirty nobles as his salary for lecturing in Greek.

He was busy all the time with translations and original work. The list of his occupations during these few years is like a summary in miniature of all his interests. In 1511, he was busy on the book he called *De Copia*, a study of richness in style and the ways of attaining it, and his advice to learners, *A Method of Study* (*De ratione studii*) was published in Paris in the same year. He was translating the Fathers: Basil's commentary on Isaiah, and St. Jerome. Simultaneously he dashed off translations of dialogues by Lucian and essays by Plutarch, as presents for his patrons. And all the time the most important work of all was going on; the collation of the Greek text of the New Testament was finished in 1513.

As usual, Erasmus was suffering from lack of money. All this work on manuscripts was expensive, and recurring illnesses were expensive too. He wrote to Ammonius in November 1513 that he was living a snail's life, shrinking inside his house and busy with study. A great solitude had been created by the plague: although, says Erasmus, it is just as lonely when they are all here. He had spent sixty nobles in the last five months, and his teaching brought him in very little. He was determined to fly away somewhere else, though where remained yet to be seen. The fact was that the great hopes with which he had come to England had not been realised. It had been a golden dream. When Mountjoy wrote his rapturous letter in 1509, inviting him to come and share in the marvellous future which was opening for humanists in England, he was obviously quite sincere. The new reign opened with enthusiasm; the King was eighteen, handsome, active, popular, interested in letters and ready to be persuaded that in encouragement of culture lay a King's chief glory. His father had left him a settled throne, by nipping off one plot after another and piling up money in the Royal treasury. All was pleasure, revels, tournaments, rejoicing. It seemed as if a famous scholar had only to appear to be fêted and provided for with a lavish hand.

In four years' time it had become abundantly clear that this was not the case. The King had been drawn into European politics, and by 1513 was invading France. If Erasmus had entertained hopes of becoming a favourite protégé of the boy he remembered meeting so long ago, he must have realised as he sat all summer in plague-stricken Cambridge unable to get any wine owing to the French wars, that his hope was not likely to come true.

All 1513 he had been on the point of taking flight. In January 1514, he left Cambridge, and in July set off on his way to Bâle, where a group of people were already working on the text of St. Jerome in conjunction with the printer Froben. Erasmus felt he must be there to take part in the work, and after a gracious (but unprofitable) audience with Henry VIII, warmly seconded by Wolsey, he left England. As he tossed on that troublesome little sea journey and eyed with distaste the cross-channel seamen whom he always declared to be the worst of robbers and rogues, his feelings must have been mixed. No doubt he had done right to resist the invitation to stay in Rome, yet all the time he had been in England the memory of Italy had assailed him: "I could not help being torn with a longing for Rome," he wrote, "whenever I recalled what I had left there—the freedom, the place itself, the light, the walks I took, the libraries I visited, the sweet converse I had with learned men, the princes of the earth who were my friends." England had been rather neglectful of him, yet it held some of his closest friends and he regarded it in a way as his adopted country. Now the scene changed, and Erasmus arrived for the first time at a city in which he was to spend half the remaining years of his life, and in which he was to die.

* * *

The New Testament

Bâle was the ideal centre from which the influence of an Erasmus could radiate. A free and independent city, it was not dominated by any great traditional power : here there was no Pope and no Sorbonne, it was not like England on the confines of Europe, or like the Netherlands, involved in the wars of the Empire. Erasmus was now becoming a European figure, and his salient characteristic of detachment

was making itself clear. All these years he had spent
in wandering from country to country, subsisting on
vague and precarious sources of income, on gifts from
the great, small profits from teaching and from books,
and latterly from the English benefice. In France, in
England, in Italy, his story had been the same: with
his heart set on one thing only, freedom to work, he
had positively avoided any kind of lucrative post that
would constitute a tie. The good old Archbishop
Warham, when allowing him to take a pension out
of the English living that he never visited, admitted
that he did not usually approve of such an arrangement, but in this case thought it right that instead of
preaching to a country congregation, Erasmus should
be spending his stipend on writing for the benefit of
all preachers. It was obvious that no post requiring
residence would ever suit Erasmus.

And now in 1514 he found his destined setting. Often
he was to leave Bâle: in fact his life continued to be a
wandering, but always he came back there, as to the
place where his unfettered and unnationalised mind
could find its free scope and true expression. From
there he could criticise the world and its masters, turn
the spotlight of his irony on the money-grubbing, the
exploiting of superstition, the abuse of power, characteristic of his time as of others, and build up for all to
see a dream of peace; sketching on the one hand
international tolerance with arbitration, rule for the
people in the people's name, on the other the practical morality of the private man, founded on knowledge, free access to the sources of Christian inspiration, deliverance from superstition and accepted
notions that had become meaningless. Erasmus was

attempting the complete reorganisation of his world, partly through comparison with the ideas of the maturer minds of the past, and partly through the inspired common sense of his own mind, having before him the ideals of the Gospel. This immense vision had grown upon him slowly, and was coming to fruition now in the years 1514–18 at Bâle. Those years placed him in his central and supreme position at the very heart of the Renaissance.

They were years of unflagging and furious industry. He found in Bâle a whole circle of new friends, centring in the printing houses of John Froben and John Amerbach, the latter of which was now being run by his two elder sons Bruno and Basil. The third son, Boniface, also became a close friend of Erasmus. It was the Amerbachs who had resolved to bring out a good edition of Jerome, and they had collected round them a team of workers, the most important being Beatus Rhenanus, afterwards Erasmus's biographer. Erasmus was cordially welcomed and deeply admired by this scholarly group, and he was naturally recognised as the main editor of the works of Jerome, while simultaneously he was enlarging the *Adagia*, revising the *Copia*, preparing an edition of Seneca, reprinting the *Enchiridion*, writing for the young Archduke Charles a treatise *On the Education of a Christian Prince*, and above all finishing his notes on the edition of the New Testament. No wonder that he refers to this spate of work as a "treadmill." It lasted from August 1514 to March 1515, (when he paid a short visit to England) and was resumed from July 1515 to May 1516. His health suffered, and he described himself in February 1516 as utterly exhausted, but it was in that month that

he wrote the preface for Froben's edition of the New
Testament. In March the book was out, "hurried
out headlong" as he says, and Erasmus's greatest
contribution to his time lay before the world.

It was not entirely without misgiving that the world
of scholarship awaited the publication of the New
Testament. The rumour ran that Erasmus was about
to publish not only the Greek text, hitherto unknown
to the printing-press, but a new Latin translation,
correcting the errors of the Vulgate. A shiver ran
through the ranks of the theologians. Correct the
received text of the Bible, the text of St. Jerome, the
text hallowed by centuries of use and veneration?
Was this not highly dangerous, and even if not, was
Erasmus of Rotterdam exactly the man to do it? It
was Martin van Dorp, a compatriot of Erasmus and
now Professor of Philosophy at Louvain, who was
bold enough (prompted by the theologians of Louvain,
who were always suspicious of Erasmus's activities)
to write to the humanist and put the objections before
him.

In the first place, he states that Erasmus had done
much harm and alienated many of his learned
friends by the rash publication of *The Praise of Folly*.
Nothing could efface the memory of this *gaffe*, unless
Erasmus were to correct the impression by writing a
Praise of Wisdom . . . And then with reference to
the New Testament: Erasmus intended to publish
the Greek text and a new translation of his own. Dorp
had two objections: Greek texts were suspect since the
alienation of the Greek world from the Church of
Rome, and the Vulgate, approved by the General
Councils of the Church, could not possibly be wrong.

Erasmus replied with the most commendable patience. He had detected sincere friendship and anxiety in the letter from Dorp, and his answer was long and exhaustive. It was easy to defend the *Moria* (*Praise of Folly*) even though he began by saying he almost regretted it in spite of the fame it had brought him. He had, however, three main lines of defence. First, he saw a continuity in his whole output, and the *Moria* was no exception: everything he had written tended to the same end, and the subject of the *Moria* was simply the subject of the *Enchiridion*, in a playful guise. Secondly, unpalatable truths are more easily digested when flavoured with laughter. Thirdly, whom had Erasmus ever attacked by name and how could anyone be offended by criticisms that were so general and free from personalities? Erasmus assured his correspondent that none of the friends he valued had been alienated, and none could be, except the ignorant hangers-on of the theological schools. (This gave him a fine opportunity for well-placed invective.)

About the New Testament, it is clear that Dorp's objections had taken his breath away. He explains that the Vulgate was clearly not Jerome's, that Jerome himself and Augustine and Ambrose all quote texts of scripture that differ from the Vulgate, that no Council ever forbade the emending of the Vulgate (characteristically he imagines a ridiculous decree of a fabulous council: "whatsoever in future, in any way, shall be corrupted, depraved, added or omitted, by any rash and half-educated, or inexperienced, or drunken, or vacillating copyists, to that do we here give our approval and authority, and let no man

74

depart therefrom"). It was not likely that the correction of a few textual errors would alienate the pious from following the footsteps of Christ.

Dorp had reminded him that others had attempted the same thing: Lorenzo Valla, the favourite author of Erasmus's youth, whose Annotations on the New Testament had shown Erasmus the way and were later edited by him, and Jacques Lefèvre d'Etaples, who had published a five-fold text of the Psalms in 1509 and a version of the Epistles of St. Paul in 1512. Erasmus agreed as to the value of these publications and added that there was still room for more. Neither he nor Dorp may have been aware that there was already in existence, printed but not published, the great Polyglot New Testament of Cardinal Ximénes, called the Complutensian. This volume confronted the Vulgate with a Greek text, but the publication was delayed by the death of the Cardinal, and it was not until 1520 that the Pope granted the licence; Erasmus did not see the Complutensian Polyglot until 1522. So his version remained technically the first in the field.

Its importance lay not in its scholarship but in what it symbolised. From the point of view of later textual criticism, Erasmus's editing was faulty to a degree. He had before him, when beginning the task in England, four Greek MSS., (which they were is now unknown) and in Bâle he had five, only one of which was either ancient or valuable. He had only one MS. of the Book of Revelation, and as it lacked the last six verses, Erasmus did not scruple to add these translated into Greek from his Latin MSS. As to printers' errors, Dr. Scrivener calls this first edition

of the New Testament "the most faulty book I know."[1]
Two workers, one of them Œcolampadius (of later
fame among the Reformers) were in charge of proof-
reading, but the haste with which the book was
tumbled out of the press did not admit of much care
in correction. Erasmus had been meditating for years
on a new Latin version of the New Testament, but
the preparation of the Greek text was done in ten
months at most, and he calls it "*praecipitatum verius
quam editum*," conscious of its many failings. In following editions (there were four in his lifetime) he
did manage to correct a good many of these faults.

If Erasmus's New Testament was hardly a sound
basis for future criticism, what placed it in its admitted key position among the most important
publications of the Renaissance?

Probably the truest answer is that it struck its
perfect hour. Educated opinion was just ready, in
1516, for such a production. To print the actual Greek
text of Scripture was to satisfy both the thirst for
Greek and the serious Christian aspirations of the
northern Renaissance; it was to point out the new
way, through widespread knowledge not confined to
a clique, towards higher moral and cultural values.
To accompany it with a new translation was to shake
off the fetters of the past and proclaim that nothing
mattered but truth—(although at first even Erasmus
was not brave enough to print his original Latin version,
written in 1506; it differed too much from the Vulgate, and it was only in the edition of 1519 that he
dared to expose all his differences of opinion with the

[1] Scrivener, *A plain introduction to the criticism of the New Testament*. London, 1894.

old text, and to print, for instance, "*In principio erat Sermo*"). The book spoke for the optimism and faith in reason of the Renaissance; Erasmus's aim was to discover the actual words written by the Apostles and their open meaning, while Lefèvre d'Etaples, representing in this instance an older outlook, would build up an elaborate allegorical significance in his treatment of the Psalms. The book, in fact, stood for the New Learning, and Erasmus, sure that his work would meet with the approval of the whole cultivated world, dedicated it boldly to the Pope, Leo X, patron of letters and the arts.

A simple way to discover just where Erasmus stood at this important juncture of his life is to analyse the famous preface to the first edition, called the *Paraclesis*. It consists of only a few pages, packed with matter, written in Erasmus's most forceful epigrammatic vein, and obviously at top speed, for it has no plan and tends to return more than once to the same line of thought. Here again Erasmus was acting the journalist, writing *tumultuarie*, even in his supremely important moment; and perhaps the sincerity of his outlook comes out clearer in these few pages because of their sense of the impromptu. Other manifestos written in haste have had the same good fortune as the *Paraclesis*, by expressing decisively the ideas of an epoch.

Erasmus began in classical vein by wishing for eloquence greater than Cicero's, to plead the cause of the Scriptures. How much care and ardour is spent on other philosophies, Platonic, Pythagorean, Stoic, Peripatetic, and so forth—how little is given to the philosophy of Christ, our author and lord! "Who would not think it disgraceful for one who professed

77

to be familiar with Aristotle's philosophy, not to know that man's opinion on the cause of lightning, on the elements, or infinity? Yet no one is the happier for knowing those things, or the unhappier for ignorance of them." And is it not worse to be ignorant of the doctrines of Christ? Indeed it is madness to compare Christ with Zeno or Aristotle, for He only is a doctor sent from heaven, and none teaches like Him. "Only He could teach with certainty, who is Eternal Wisdom." Why are we not more curious about knowledge which has been brought to us from so far. and such knowledge that it makes any wisdom of this world look like stupidity? And when it is to be found with so little trouble, in so few books? For this learning is of a special kind.

"For it is not necessary that you should come to it prepared by so much anxious training; it is there, provision for your journey, simple and ready to hand for all . . . Only be teachable, and you will make great strides in this philosophy. Itself will supply you with a teacher, the Spirit, who imparts himself to none more readily than to the simple of heart . . . This philosophy, unlike others, suits itself equally to all; it stoops to the small, tempers itself to their littleness, suckles and carries them, cherishes and sustains them, doing all for us until we grow up in Christ. It is within reach of the lowest, just as it is the admiration of the greatest; and indeed, the further you progress in knowledge of its treasures, the more you will be moved by the sense of its majesty . . . It rejects no one, of any age, sex, means or condition. The sun itself is not as common to all as the teaching of Christ."

For this reason, Erasmus disagrees strongly with those who do not wish to see the Scriptures translated into the vulgar tongue, for the ordinary person to read, as if Christ taught such complicated things that only a theologian here and there could understand them, or as if the safety of the Christian religion lay in its not being understood. In a famous passage Erasmus expresses his passionate feeling on the subject: "I wish that all women might read the Gospel, and the Epistles of Paul. I wish that they might be translated into all tongues of all people, so that not only the Scots and the Irish, but also the Turk and the Saracen might read and understand. I wish the countryman might sing them at his plough, the weaver chant them at his loom, the traveller beguile with them the weariness of his journey." Why should we regard as the privilege of a few (and those not always devout or unworldly) what is in reality the common possession of us all? "Him do I count a true divine," says the quaint English translation of 1529[1], "which not with craftye and sotle reasons, but in harte, countenance, eyes and lyffe doth teach to despyse riches: and that a Christian ought not to put confidence in the sucker and helpe of this worlde, but only whole to hang on heven; not to avenge injurye, to pray for them that say evyll by us, to do good agaynst evyll . . . yf eny man beynge inspired with the holy ghoste do prech and teach these and soch other things, yf eny man exhorte, entyse and bolden his neighbour unto these things, he ys a very and true

---

[1] *An exhortation to the diligent study of scripture, made by Erasmus Rotterodamus, and translated into inglissh.* At Marborrow in the lond of Hesse. MD XXIX (Hans Luft).

divine, though he be a wever, yea though he digge and delve. But he that accomplissheth and fulfylleth these thinges in his liffe and maners, he verely is a great doctor."

It may seem that these things are humble and illiterate beside the disputations of the schools, and yet these are what Christ taught, and His Apostles. The "rude multitude" may be comforted, because the Apostles taught such things, and not the subtle arguments of the schools (whether they knew the latter or not, says Erasmus wickedly, I leave others to judge). These things, the simple doctrine of Christ, is what should be dispensed by those in authority to do so, and they are principally of three classes—rulers, preachers and teachers of the young. If these three kinds of men were to act on and spread the true precepts of Christ, then quietness would be restored to Christendom and Christians would differ from the heathen in more than name.

Here Erasmus turns back over his previous arguments, and repeats some of them; he goes on to suggest how far the ancient philosophers are in concordance with the Philosophy of Christ, how Stoics, Epicureans, Socrates and Aristotle have all declared beliefs that are part of Christ's teaching. But of all teachers Christ taught these things best. The first thing, therefore, is to find out what he taught, the next is to act on it. *Primum autem est scire quid docuerit, proximum est praestare.* Why choose any other source of knowledge? There are other avenues of approach (e.g. the intricacies of the Schoolmen) but it is the Gospel which yields the "true and natural philosophy of Christ." But it must be read with prayer rather than disputation, and with the desire to be transformed rather than to acquire intellectual weapons.

In conclusion, Erasmus plays back and forth on two themes familiar from the *Enchiridion*: (1) We preserve our friends' letters, and the Orders—Augustinian, Benedictine, Franciscan—treasure their Rule; why do not all Christians treasure the Scriptures? (2) The image of Christ contained in the Gospel is much more real and precious than any material relics of Him that could be found. "Insomuch that thou couldste not so playne and fruitefully see him, all though he were presente before thy bodily eyes."

In these few simple arguments lie embedded the representative ideas of Erasmus, those which were most potent over his own time, and which link up his work most surely with past, present and future. The *Paraclesis* became famous, and rightly so, as it is almost a summary of Erasmus's contribution to the Renaissance. Three main lines of significance can be selected in illustration of this.

In the first place, the whole preface is redolent of humanism—it breathes the true optimism of the Renaissance. The very expression he coined, *philosophia Christi*, speaks of an aspect of religion which appeals first to the mind. Confidence in knowledge, and knowledge attained and explored by reason, is the keynote: evidently it is taken for granted that if the words of Christ were sufficiently known and studied, the course of the world would be altered and the abuses put right. The first thing is to know and the second to act, and the one follows closely on the other as a natural consequence. Erasmus does not work this out as a theory like Descartes, but he is not far from the same serene assurance. He writes in passing a revealing sentence about the nature of man: "Now doth every mannes mynd incline unto that which is wholesome and expedient for his nature. And what other thinge ys this doctrine of Christ which he calleth the new regeneracyon, but a restoringe or reparynge of oure nature which in hys fyrst creacyon was good?" This illustrates well the "shelving" process by which Erasmus, who disliked theorising, managed to subscribe to two opposing views at once. He accepts the doctrine of the Fall and the faultiness of man's perverted nature, but being a humanist, he prefers to lay stress on the potentialities for good that also exist in the nature of man, and to see him as thirsting for an experience which will bring him back to his pristine state of goodness. This emphasis on the powers and potentialities of mankind is essentially humanistic, but Erasmus manages to hold it and remain a Christian, thus maintaining his central position between the pagan humanists rejoicing in their confidence in man's native powers and goodness, and the Lutheran and Calvinist denying to man any virtues of his own at all. Erasmus did not work out this position either: only a Pascal could demonstrate the way to a true harmony between these two interpretations of man's place and destiny, by showing how his dual nature makes him akin to the highest and lowest at one and the same time. For Erasmus, disliking logic and intent on practical ends, it was enough to have faith in the power of the understanding, and he thought it worth while to point out also how much of pagan philosophy had foreshadowed the teaching of Jesus. True to his own teaching in the *Enchiridion*, Erasmus sees the revealed philosophy of Christ as the peak and crown of all wisdom, and salutes, leading up to it, the many paths discovered of old in the half-light of the ancient world.

But in spite of his faith in the powers of the mind, Erasmus cannot fairly be called a rationalist. He had a deep distrust of intellectual subtlety, and here, in the work of his maturity, we can trace the flowering of those seeds sown long ago in the schools of the Brethren of the Common Life. The wisdom he is writing of is the wisdom that "is from on high," and it needs qualities of heart as well as of mind. This is implicit in all that Erasmus says in favour of putting the Scriptures into the hands of the simplest people, for they may be nearer a true understanding of it than the most complicated brains. Much of what he says— that intellectual discussion and "craftye and sotle reasons" are valueless here, that the Apostles did not deal in the science of the Schoolmen, that this kind of learning is better approached with prayer than with argument, that it is "a life rather than a disputation, an inspiration rather than a science, a regeneration rather than a reasoning"—all this is to be found in the pages of *The Imitation of Christ*, little changed, if at all. It is surprising at first to find Erasmus, of all people, laying stress on a mode of understanding that is not purely rational. And yet that dislike of abstract argument had always been a characteristic of his: with all his reasons for undervaluing the Brethren and their ideals, he had always recognised that he and they had the same enemies, the mental gymnasts of medieval philosophy. And though Erasmus could no more be called a mystic than a rationalist, it is in keeping with his character that he should occupy a middle position between the two. Both the rational method and the more direct spiritual grasp are necessary, and faith completes the work of reason, just as Christ's teaching lets in a flood of light on the groping of the classical moralists. In this kind of learning alone, he says, reverence steps in where reason is brought to a standstill: *in his solis literis, et quod non assequor, tamen adoro.*

The third significant fact about the arguments of the *Paraclesis* is that they were almost all to become the arguments of the Reformers. Although, in the future, Erasmus was to feel deeply the existence of the gulf that separated him from Luther, and to say so in no uncertain terms, it was several years after the appearance of Luther before that gulf became evident. For some contemporaries it was never evident at all, and the traditionalists are to be excused if they lumped together Erasmus and the Reformers in one wholesale condemnation. The separation and final open antagonism between the ideals of the reformers and those of the humanists was a process covering a number of years, and perhaps it was not until 1536, the year in which Calvin's *Institution* saw the light and Erasmus died, that the deep-seated differences between the two attitudes of mind became plain. Even then, Erasmus was regarded by those in favour of Reform as having drawn back from his earlier boldness, having looked back after putting his hand to the plough, whereas the truth was that he had never altered his position since the publication of the *Enchiridion*. The world changed round him, but he remained stubbornly faithful to that most difficult of positions to defend, a middle way. That his consistency should be easily mistaken for vacillation illustrates the complicated nature of the individualistic attitude he had chosen to preserve. The questions in which he disagreed with the Reformers were mainly fundamental ones; those on which he agreed were practical issues affecting the conduct of society and daily life, and it was natural that the similarities between his outlook and Luther's should at first be more in evidence than the divergences. At all events, the *Paraclesis* may be taken to represent a period in which Humanism (in northern Europe) and the dawn of the Reformation appear to be strongly united, to champion the same causes and rely on the same weapons. Almost all the ideas expressed in the *Paraclesis* were in accordance with those later expressed by Luther: the claim that the Bible was common to all men, the wish for it to be available to the simple, and translated into the common tongue, the assertion that the true priest is he who preaches Christian doctrine and practises it "though he be a wever, yea though he digge and delve," and finally the argument carried on from the *Enchiridion*, that the spiritual inheritance of the earthly life of Christ and his saints is far more valuable than any material relics that could possibly be found—all these tenets are common to Erasmus and the Reformers. So much was this the case, that when in 1534, the younger Cop, son of Erasmus's doctor, wished to make a revolutionary inaugural speech as Rector of the University of Paris and called in his friend Jean Calvin to help, the result was a neat dovetailing of the *Paraclesis* and Luther's doctrine of justification by faith, and the combination surprised nobody. In the *Paraclesis* and in some of his satirical writings Erasmus seemed to express before-hand many of the thoughts nearest to the heart of the Reformers.

85

Chapter Three

The World Through Erasmus's Eyes: Humour and Satire

UP to this point we have followed Erasmus step by step in his wanderings, and have witnessed his efforts to gain status, and to keep body and soul together, without sacrificing his freedom or renouncing the "golden rivers" of Greek. We have accompanied him to what R. W. Chambers, the biographer of Thomas More, calls "the golden year of Erasmian reform," the year 1516. From now onward our method will be a different one; we shall attempt to study his thought rather than to follow his movements, for it would be tedious, in so short a study, to give a close account of his journeyings during the next twenty years. They were less varied than before. There is abundant evidence that Erasmus never felt static, that he was as restless in his latter years as in the long period of his development; he was always making plans to move on somewhere else. But after 1516 it was not so easy, for two main reasons: a growing tendency to illness, which often made him postpone his plans, and, more important still, the new conditions imposed by the growth of the Reformation. The vision of a peaceful Republic of Letters was a fading dream, and one after another the avenues closed, as one milieu after another grew too bitter in the controversy to look kindly on the leader of thought who refused to take sides. Erasmus spent the last twenty years of his life mainly between Louvain (till it grew too hot to hold him), Bâle, and Freiburg in Breisgau. He dallied with the thought of visiting other countries, especially Italy, but expediency kept him for the most part in his central bastion, looking out on a warring Europe.

His situation was now clear. The kindness with which the Pope, Leo X, had received the dedication of his New Testament, emboldened Erasmus to ask for a dispensation which would place him in complete security to pursue his life of authorship. Hitherto he had been haunted by the ills of his childhood and youth; all through the Paris period, and after, he had kept warily in touch with his monastery, feeling obliged to write periodically to the Prior and explain what work he was doing and why he was still absent. He had ceased to wear the dress of an Augustinian canon, since a day in Bologna when he had been stoned by a crowd which mistook him for a plague doctor; this incident may well have really happened as he describes it, but surely the fundamental reason for his adopting the ordinary dress of a secular cleric was his profound distaste for all that pertained to the monastic life. Now he was famous, and there was little left to connect him with the dark and tragic circumstances of his early life in Holland; but the insecurity remained, increased by Erasmus's private knowledge that he had no right, owing to his illegitimate birth, to accept the benefices which were offered to him. Financial independence, liberty of body and mind, fame and leisure, were all within his grasp, prizes coveted for a lifetime; but he was legally ineligible for the benefices, subject to ecclesiastical penalties for having discarded his habit and thus broken his vows, and in danger of the appalling fate of being recalled to Steyn.

Negotiation through his friend Ammonius, the Papal delegate in England, brought him security at last, in the form of two dispensations, one a letter addressed to himself from the Pope, which absolved him in general terms and which he could show to all comers, the other a letter from the Pope to Ammonius, with a much more specific reference to the illegitimate birth of the unnamed appellant. This was a piece of tact which corresponded with the evasive manner of Erasmus's application, through the curious letter to a fictitious "Lambertus Grunnius" describing the pressure put upon his brother and himself to enter the monastic life: they are referred to by substituted names as Florentius and Antonius. It was not till later, in 1524, that he wrote the account of his birth and early years which has since become famous.

Erasmus went to England in the spring of 1517, and received his absolution on April 9th at the hands of Ammonius, by a formal ceremony which took place in Ammonius's house at Westminster—one of the Canon's houses of St. Stephen's, on the site of which, later on, was built the House of Commons.

In 1515, he had been appointed a Councillor of the Empire, a post which carried with it a yearly salary, and in 1516 a canonry of Courtrai had been offered to him. The latter had been commuted to a pension, as Erasmus had no intention of fulfilling the duties of a Canon; and he was now not only safe, but for the first time in possession of moderate means to relieve him of the lifelong anxiety as to where his next year's subsistence was to come from. The programme in front of him was still as large, it increased with his labours as such visions do instead of abating, but enough of it lay realised behind him to justify some confidence. There is a certain authority in his expression as he sits at his desk in Metsys' painting of 1517 (sent to More as a present, with a companion portrait of their mutual friend Peter Gilles), and a sense of determination in the set lips. (Erasmus was amused at his own portraits, and said of Holbein's sketch of him on the margins of *The Praise of Folly*— "If Erasmus still looked like that, he would take a wife at once!")

An extract from a letter from Cambridge written in 1516[1] will serve to illustrate the position Erasmus had now achieved in the world of learning. The writer was John Watson, Fellow of Peterhouse from 1501–17 but just returned from Italy. After congratulating Erasmus on his court appointment to Prince Charles, and thanking him for his letter "valued by me," says Watson, "almost as much as the best living that could be given me—now I can imagine you laughing and saying : ' 'Tis honest of you to add *almost*!' "—the letter goes on —"I am constantly more and more impressed, when I see Erasmus growing greater as he advances in years, and showing himself every day in a new and more exalted character. You are celebrated everywhere in Italy, especially among the learned of the highest note. It is incredible, how favourably your *Copia* is everywhere received; and

[1] Nichols, op. cit. II., p. 333.

your *Folly* regarded as the highest wisdom. I met many persons who seemed to me to think themselves more learned, because they were among your acquaintance, and with whom I was myself in higher esteem on that account . . . Your fame is spread throughout all the Christian world; but as others enlarge on the riches of your varied learning or extraordinary eloquence, nothing strikes me so much as the modesty with which you are ready to take the lowest place, while the general suffrage sets you in the highest. The kind of literary skill which you enjoy is apt to inflate the possessor of it, and as it puts him in a peculiar class, to separate him from familiarity with his kind; but you are all generosity in communicating yourself to others; and having for your object the welfare of all, you do not despise the friendship of any. Therefore, wherever you are, you so live as to seem present everywhere in Christendom, and will continue to live by the immortality of your fame and the noble monuments you will leave behind you."

The particular praise selected by Watson shows an acute appreciation of Erasmus's peculiar powers. It was because he remained so much in contact with others, because he showed so much imagination in visualising the lives and needs of ordinary people, and in bringing to their door the fruits of hardly won learning that he was different from the other scholars of his day. To some, especially among the Renaissance poets, it was the fashion to adopt an exclusive attitude with the *Odi profanum vulgus* of Horace as their banner. Erasmus on the contrary, was a "vulgariser" like Voltaire, with whom he has often been compared; but there is an important difference, for while Voltaire intended to destroy and had little that was fundamental to offer in place of what he destroyed, Erasmus attempted to put within reach of the people a positive creed, and the riches of many other minds besides his own. Yet he was fastidious and critical. His relationship with the world outside his study is a complicated one, because it shares in that duality which we have already noticed in his works. He loved distinction of mind, and also loved simplicity. The Erasmus who worshipped learning and proclaimed the right of reason to its own judgment, and yet feared and despised intellectual subtlety, is the same Erasmus as we find calling the Cambridge carriers and the Channel boatmen by the hardest of names, refusing to use any vernacular, and generally drawing his cloak round him with a fastidious gesture, and yet writing in the tenderest and most understanding vein about the lives of girls, boys, mothers and simple men.

We have already seen something of the serious basis for his contemporary fame. But it rested quite as much on his humorous writings, and as time has flowed on these have become much more important in comparison with his tremendous output of learned work. If Erasmus survives today, it is largely owing to the undying qualities of the *Colloquies* and *The Praise of Folly*. What did these books mean to his contemporaries; why do they permeate the subsequent literature of the Renaissance, and how far do they remain alive for us today?

(a) "THE PRAISE OF FOLLY"

When Erasmus was riding over the Alps amusing himself with reflections on what he had seen, there

came to his mind a famous satire published some years
before at Bâle; the *Ship of Fools*[1] of Sebastian
Brant. On Brant's ship there were collected 112 different kinds of fools, and the portrayal of them gave
infinite scope for satirical description, and for delighted recognition by the reader. The popularity of
this book was immense, and it was recognised as a
salutary fable into the bargain. It had been published
in German in 1494, in French and Latin in following
years. Erasmus must have read one of the Latin
versions of Brant's book, probably the 1505 one as he
was in relations with the printer Josse Bade, and
possibly the idea of a comprehensive study of the
folly of mankind sprang from this source. But he did
not in any sense imitate it. His fancy ran to a more
classical type of satire; he saw Folly in her cap and
bells ascending the pulpit of the orator, looking round
on her audience and noticing how they all cheered
up at the very sight of her, before she launched out
into a declamation in proper rhetorical style. The
very conception was a tribute to friendship. Erasmus
was hurrying towards England; his mind went faster
than his horse's feet, and the thought of his friend
Thomas More, whom he was soon to see again, and
the atmosphere of the new home in the City (to which
More had taken his young wife the year before
Erasmus's departure for Italy) came to meet him with
strong actuality. He thought, so he says, how like

[1] See H. M. Allen, introduction to *The Praise of Folly*, Oxford,
1913 (the translation used here). The idea of a review of the
different forms of human life, by rank, age and profession is a
familiar one in the fifteenth century, and Brant was perhaps
only applying in a comic and satirical vein the method of the
Danse Macabre.

More's name was the name of Folly (Moria) and how distant More was from the thing. And out of this little joke sprang the magisterial declamations of Folly herself.

It is worth remarking here how the character of More is intertwined with all Erasmus's humorous writings. It was a friendship without a shadow; R. W. Chambers notes very justly that whereas a note of irritation often creeps into Erasmus's letters to Colet, there is never the slightest hint of it in his letters to More, and Erasmus was not always free from touchiness with his friends. But with More, that almost perfect character, gentle, resolute, with funds of human sympathy and inextinguishable laughter, he had the closest of bonds, an identical sense of humour. No doubt his restless, sensitive spirit found rest in More's unshakeable friendship and integrity. Only one other recorded friendship of Erasmus's had been founded on laughter, and that was with the Italian poet in Paris, Fausto Andrelini. But Erasmus knew well that character in Fausto's case left much to be desired. With More, the bond of friendship had everything to adorn it, and it is pleasant to think of the week's holiday that constituted the writing of *The Praise of Folly*, in More's Bucklersbury home, which was then at its gayest time; More, a rising young lawyer, was high in favour with the new King, and happy with his young wife and his four tiny children, of whom the last, his only son John, had just been born. It was a happiness that was soon interrupted by the death of the first Mistress More, whom her husband always remembered with tenderness; in his own epitaph, which he wrote many years later, he called her *cara uxorcula*, his darling little wife. Such a household Erasmus may well have envied, debarred as he was from family life; but Erasmus, unlike More, had not had the liberty to sit down and meditate on his own character and fitness for celibacy or marriage.

The book he produced in these pleasant surroundings must have been somewhat of a surprise to himself. It was one of those trifles tossed off in a short time which reveal better than anything else the character and intentions of the writer.

The *Moria* falls into three sections, very unequal in length, and quite different in intention, though they are linked together by skilful transitions and the prevalence of the same bantering tone. Roughly they may be classed as follows:

(a) Folly introduces herself; a light-hearted attribution of all good things in life to Folly;

(b) A satiric attack on current abuses, and especially on the people and activities that Erasmus most disliked;

(c) A few mysterious pages in which the intention is apparently neither comic nor satirical, but with a much deeper sense.

The first two sections are easy to understand; it was the last which produced adverse comment and puzzled Erasmus's contemporaries.

The opening part of Folly's speech is really masterly fooling. It is gay and carefree, a scholar's joke in impeccable classical style, and as such it no doubt pleased everybody and made no enemies. Folly turns out to be quite well-read, and knows how authors in the past have written panegyrics of agues,

94

flies, baldness and such other pests of nature; therefore why should she not extol herself? Nothing could
be more in character, and the way in which she dis-
claims any intention of behaving like a rhetorician
and opening her speech with a definition, then goes
on to describe her origins with a closeness that equals
any definition ever made, is charmingly in keeping
with herself. Folly in this part of her discourse is
really much more than mere foolishness: she is
unquenchable animal spirits, the gaiety of youth, the
irrational element in mankind, which makes us fall
in love, have children, be merry in our childhood
and youth; even the classical gods came under her
spell, and Folly paints a merry picture, rather like
a turbulent painted ceiling of the Renaissance, depicting all the gods of Olympus giving way to Folly. It
is clear from this that Folly here represents all the
qualities and all the activities of life which are outside
the pale of reason. She finds it easy to prove that the
motives which bring about great deeds, such as
courage in war and the love of glory, are folly rather
than wisdom, that a mob which will not listen to
wise counsel will be moved by a childish fable, that
Folly laid the foundation of cities, and that by her
"Empire, Authority, Policy and publique Actions
are preserved; neither is there anything in Human
Life that is not a kind of pastime of Folly."

The whole of this argument mounts up to a profound conclusion closely related to the thought of
Montaigne and of Pascal: namely, that human
society largely depends for its existence on the
accepting by a large number of people of certain
appearances or conventions, which are seen as Folly

by the truly wise man, but " 'tis the part of a truly Prudent man not to be wise beyond his condition." These conventions are essential for the conduct of life.

This part of Folly's sermon concludes with a sketch of the origins of happiness, (which is according to her, mainly delusion), and a rough classification of the different types of fools who enjoy her consoling bounty; thus she passes from the general to the particular, and embarks on the ironical review of the world's foolishness which constitutes the second section of the book.

And here the character of the speaker begins to change. An element of criticism comes in, and Folly is no longer the genial source of life's brightness, but something much nearer the general acceptation of her name. At the beginning of the list of fools, she merely makes people ridiculous, but at the end she makes them criminal. Naturally the most severe criticism falls on Erasmus's own pet aversions, worthless monks, vain Schoolmen and warring Popes, and such is his hatred of their unlikeness to their Christian profession that Folly nearly drops her bantering tone to turn on them with fury. The serious nature of the book is clear in these pages, and one understands why Erasmus could say that in the *Moria* he was doing exactly the same thing as in the *Enchiridion*, though in a different way: he was indeed broadcasting the same message, that we should look to realities rather than to names, to a man's life rather than to his words, to the spirit rather than to the letter of the law. But he had more confidence and more experience now than when he wrote the *Enchiridion*; and no serious book could ever have the

sting or the brilliant satire of the *Moria*. The shafts
went home in quite a different way.

It is the fate of all satirical writing to change in
interest as the years go by, as different facets of the
irony are caught by the light of rising and setting
suns. To us the general picture is interesting, painted
with merry humour rather than with a pen dipped
in gall. We are amused to know that in the early
sixteenth century it was the English who prided themselves on their music, their beauty and their banquets,
the Scotch who vaunted their high descent and their
subtle Schoolmen, the Parisians who thought themselves unique as students of divinity, the Italians, not
unnaturally, who claimed to be the only masters of
learning and eloquence and despised all other nations
as barbarous. There are innumerable touches in *The
Praise of Folly* which either illustrate amusingly the
foibles of a bygone age, or shed a passing light on a
permanent human weakness which we recognise as
of our world of today. But to Erasmus's contemporaries the parts of deepest interest in Folly's
utterances must have been those which threw into
relief the specific abuses of their own time—the
pages in which Erasmus took his long-desired fling
at the successors of the Schoolmen, and by his
comical selection of their "Magisterial Definitions,
Conclusions, Corollaries, Propositions Explicit and
Implicit," dealt the dying science such a blow that it
constitutes a *coup de grâce*; or those where the long
procession of ignorant and conceited monks winds in
front of our mental vision, with their meticulous
observance of tiny rules concerning dress, as to the
number of knots in shoe-strings or girdle, width of

97

cowl or colour of habit, and their utter disregard of purity of life or the example of the Apostles. Erasmus really enjoyed himself here. He was fervently working for the reform of Christendom, and he was also avenging years of humiliation in which he had been forced to watch what he describes, and ostensibly to identify himself with it. This perhaps accounts for the specially bitter tone in which he always speaks of the trivialities of the monastic life. Here he draws a picture of the Last Judgment, at which an endless variety of monks bring accounts of their doings which merit Heaven: one shows a trough full of fish, another so many bushels of prayers, another brags of not having touched a penny for sixty years *without at least two pairs of gloves on*, another that he has lived for fifty-five years like a sponge, always fixed to the same place . . . and so on. But Christ answers them, "There is only one law which is truly mine, and of that I hear nothing."

Folly has something to say of princes and court lords, but she warms up again when it comes to reviewing her share in the lives of Bishops, Cardinals and Popes. It is in her condemnation of the un-apostolic activities of warlike Popes, such as Erasmus had observed with passionate indignation in Italy, that his eloquence rises to its height. The Papal court, with its pomp and trappings, its crowd of hangers-on, guards, clerks, notaries, muleteers, bankers, comes vividly back before his mind, and in the centre of this luxury the soldierly figure of Julius II. He makes Folly dare to say that through her alone, Popes live more voluptuously and with less trouble than almost any other kind of men, thinking that

98

Christ will be well enough pleased if they act as bishops in title and ceremony only.

"As if the Church had any deadlier enemies than wicked Prelates, who not only suffer Christ to run out of request for want of preaching him, but hinder his spreading by their multitudes of Laws, merely contrived for their own profit, corrupt him by their forced Expositions, and murder him by the evil example of their pestilent life."

A bold utterance from a runaway monk in 1509. But when Leo X read the *Moria*, he only laughed and said: "I am glad our Erasmus is in the *Moria* himself." And so he is, cited at the end among the authorities in Biblical criticism, for Folly sets up as a doctor herself and quotes texts to show her own worth and value.

And here the character of Folly begins to change again. Under the influence of the texts of Scripture, such as "the preaching of the Cross is to them that perish foolishness", a different aspect of Folly comes into sight; she has already changed from something which amounted to a life-force into the blind self-love of deluded mankind, and now her Protean character melts into yet another shape, the self-forgetfulness of the mystics and the saints. The link between all three aspects is that they are all outside the pale of Reason; but as we have already seen, Erasmus was only up to a point an admirer of Reason. Only a reader who took him to be a whole-hearted rationalist could imagine that in these last pages he was mocking at sacred things, when he allows Folly to speak of the preference shown by Jesus for simple people, children and women and fishermen, or when she paints the mystic trance

99

as a foretaste of Heaven. These pages did indeed alarm certain sober-minded contemporaries, and to a later taste they may be unexpected and doubtful, mingling as they do sacred things with profane. But to those who understood Erasmus's character and drift, as More, for instance, must have done, there could have been no ambiguity.

Two considerations may help here to come to an understanding of Erasmus's purpose. One is that the sixteenth-century writer did sometimes employ this technique, which was useful to him because it acted both as a disguise and a challenge. A good example is found in the chapters of the *Quart Livre* of *Pantagruel* (LVII–LXII), in which Rabelais describes the visit of Pantagruel and his friends, in the course of their wanderings, to the territory of Messer Gaster and his subjects the Gastolatres; Gaster appears to symbolise at one point human greed, at another economic necessity. Erasmus's Folly perhaps gave Rabelais a model for his swift change and counterchange in tone. An insubstantial goddess, she switches insidiously from one character to another; whatever she may say can immediately be excused because it proceeds out of the mouth of Folly, and her irrational behaviour in now forgetting and now remembering who she is, is distractingly in keeping with her personality.

Secondly, Erasmus's other writings illuminate his purpose here. As we have seen, the irony of the second part of the *Moria* need not lead us to suppose that when he allowed his Folly to describe the raptures of the mystics, Erasmus was either satirising them or cracking a bad joke. On the contrary, the meaning of this "true word spoken in jest" seems to be strictly

in accordance with the message of the *Enchiridion* and
the *Paraclesis*, in fact, with that side of Erasmus's outlook which we have partly traced back to the teaching
of the Brethren of the Common Life: the distrust of
the intellect, and the condemnation of intellectual
pride. The propositions of Folly are inconsequent, as
becomes her, but beneath the manner, which is preserved to the end, there is a serious respect for the
supra-rational, the wisdom which has nothing to do
with reasoning or calculation and, therefore, may be
akin to Folly, the unworldliness which takes its models
from children, lilies, sparrows and mustard-seed, for
it belongs to the kingdom of Heaven. The behaviour
of the Christian is utter foolishness in the eyes of
Mr. Worldly Wiseman: and the saint in contemplation is lost to the world of common sense. He is
ravished in soul like a lover, and the more complete
his self-forgetfulness, the greater his foretaste of
Heaven.

"For as much as the life of holy men is nothing but
a continued meditation and, as it were, shadow of that
life, it so happens that at length they have some taste
or relish of it; which, though it be but as the smallest
drop in comparison of that fountain of eternal happiness, yet it far surpasses all worldly delight, though all
the pleasures of mankind were all joyn'd together. So
much better are things spiritual than things corporal,
and things invisible than things visible . . ." This is
the very keynote of the climax of the *Enchiridion*.

And so ends *The Praise of Folly*, with perfect sym-
metry, making the unreason of the mystic at the end
respond to the unreason of the lover or the child at the
beginning. And here it may be remarked in passing

that there is a curious resemblance between these three phases of *The Praise of Folly* and the three Orders whose discovery as a law of the universe so haunted Pascal. The point of similarity is that for Pascal the natural ignorance of the common people, constituting the first Order, and the inspired comprehension of the saint, constituting the third, often touch, especially in their attitude to worldly things. What then? Are we to conclude that Erasmus forestalled Pascal, or that Pascal was inspired by Erasmus? Manifestly neither is true. But we can conclude two things from this unexpected conjunction: that the influence of one spirit on another in the European tradition of thought (as of Erasmus on Montaigne and Montaigne on Pascal) is closer and more far-reaching than appears at first; and secondly, that for Erasmus to be dubbed a sceptic and a rationalist, on the score of *The Praise of Folly*, was a strange misreading of the facts, since he comes here into close sympathy with the greatest exponent of the relationship between reason and the intuition of the mystic.

(b) THE "COLLOQUIES"

The *Colloquies* of Erasmus are one of the great books of the Renaissance. As one of their most devoted friends has said: "If literary theft be, like imitation, one of the sincerest forms of flattery, the *Colloquies* of Erasmus occupy the proud position of one of the most pillaged works in existence."[1] They not only rejoiced the heart of their own generation, they were read throughout the sixteenth century and far beyond, and

[1] Preserved Smith, *A Key to the Colloquies of Erasmus*, Harvard University Press, 1927.

have acted as a quarry of humorous anecdote and local colour for fiction and drama up to our own time. In the sixteenth century, the list of borrowers from them includes such names as Shakespeare and Ben Jonson, Montaigne and Cervantes, Rabelais, Clément Marot, Marguerite de Navarre. Later, Molière and possibly even Pascal remembered them, and in the nineteenth century it was not surprising that Sir Walter Scott should turn to them in his search for descriptive detail of the past. The use made of them by Charles Reade in *The Cloister and the Hearth* is well known, but it is strange to find among their debtors Victorien Sardou. Probably many other traces of their influence could be found by a determined search, for they must have been one of the most widely read books ever written.

It is particularly in reading the *Colloquies* that we allow ourselves to regret Erasmus's fidelity to Latin: his easy fluency and witty conciseness are so apt to vanish under a translator's hand, and humour, like Vouvray, suffers in transit. And yet not only did the *Colloquies'* Latin dress allow them to have a wider influence in their day than would otherwise have been possible, but they owe their very inception to the interest of their author in the correct teaching of Latin. When Erasmus was a poor student in Paris, obliged to take a few pupils for the sake of earning his bread, he wrote a number of dialogues for them, to illustrate forms of speech and address and to familiarise them with the use of Latin as the language of everyday life. Through these first dialogues recur the names of his Paris friends and the students whom he taught there: Christian Northoff, Peter Gilles, Thomas

Grey, James Maurice of Gouda, Francis Theodoric, Cornelius Gerard, Richard Arnold, Fausto Andrelini. One of them was an acquaintance whose activity in the bookselling line was useful to Erasmus, but for whom as a person he never cared: Augustine Vincent Caminade. This man appears to have given readings of new books in booksellers' shops (the contemporary form of advertisement) and was entrusted by Erasmus with some literary business. Long afterwards, in 1518, Augustine Caminade collected the Latin dialogues by Erasmus he possessed, and published them without the author's knowledge. This was often a transparent literary device, but in this case Erasmus's anger was quite genuine, and he hurried into print an authentic and more correct version (1519). This was the *Familiorum Colloquiorum Formulae*. In 1522, he brought out a much enlarged edition printed by Froben, and dedicated to Froben's little son Erasmius. This was the basis for the many subsequent editions, enlarged each time by the addition of new Colloquies, until three years before the author's death in 1536. The book which began as a few practical hints and "formulae," ended as the *Colloquiorum Opus*, containing over sixty Colloquies, many of them complete stories or one-act dramas and full of incident, personal opinions, acute psychological observation, detail and colour.

The book which was thus nearly forty years in the making can be compared in some ways to Montaigne's *Essais*. Like them, it grew from a short and formal exercise, in which the author acted more as a collector of material than as a creator, and it expanded into a highly original form of literature which expressed the

104

author's deepest preoccupations and interests. But there the resemblance ends, for while the originality of Montaigne lay in his investigation of his own personality by favour of his retirement from the world, Erasmus's thought was continually directed outwards, in perpetual contact with the events of his time, commenting, criticising, attempting to influence by ridicule or by protest, exposing abuses or building up an ideal. The personality of the author is never absent, but it is involved in the active dramatic life of the speakers and their friends.

The *Colloquies* are an all-purpose book. Apart from their initial pedagogic intention (which assured their use as a schoolbook for many years, in spite of various attempts to ban them as unorthodox), they were a running commentary on current events, in which Erasmus could indulge his learning towards journalism; they belong in a way to the broadsheet class of literature which preceded the newspaper. In them, under cover of fictitious names and an apparently impersonal form, he could express his own ideas, follow the course of political or religious quarrels, discuss burning topics of the day at Bâle, recommend ways of living, from ethics to hygiene, attack his enemies and the enemies of sound learning, defend his friends and on occasion himself. Like both Montaigne and Rabelais, Erasmus realised in the course of writing what varied purposes could be served by the apparently simple form of literature he had embarked upon, and raised it to the status of a classic.

All these purposes were utilitarian. But Erasmus was not only a Latin scholar and a corrector of morals. He was a most human person, with an incurably frivolous side; he had a delight in the ridiculous, an acute eye, a knowledge of character and a sympathy with natural ways of living. The *Colloquies* are the only work of his (except his letters) in which all these qualities can find their full expression. They make the book into one of the richest and most crowded canvases depicting the life of the Renaissance.

On the whole the picture shown us is of the 1520's. As we have seen, some of the *Colloquies* were in existence long before, and some were still being added in 1533, but the great bulk of them appeared during 1523–8. They date from a period of maximum activity in Erasmus's life, when he was recognised as the greatest scholar in Europe, and as having a voice of authority; but also when he was resolutely avoiding the dangers of entanglement in the Lutheran controversy, which was sweeping Europe into war; and when he was beginning to fend off the attacks of critics and enemies which were to pursue him to the end of his life. The *Colloquies* can thus be roughly divided into three types, though some of the greatest partake of all three characters: there are the stylistic ones, directed to literary uses; the polemical ones, holding up to ridicule and scorn the abuses of the day, and defending the author; and those which illustrate some characteristic attitude of the Renaissance, or describe graphically what it was like to be alive in 1526, or tell entertaining stories, or paint an ideal picture such as always lingered at the back of Erasmus's mind.

Even the purely stylistic exercises have a flavour of their time. Not for nothing did Erasmus write *De Copia*. Some of the early conversations such as the one

between Pamphagus and Cocles, discussing the varied
uses that could be made of Cocles' nose, are in the
exuberant vein which was carried to such lengths by
Rabelais. Style, to the men of the early Renaissance,
meant not only finding the right word, but rejoicing
in a torrent of words, playing with them and tossing
them in the air. It is said that Erasmus, so cautious
in his letters and most of his writings, was highly
indiscreet in his talk, and in the *Colloquies* we have an
echo of his readiness of tongue as well as his biting
wit. Other stylistic exercises include a classical imitation in which a young man holds a conversation with
an echo, the last syllables of his question always being
contrived to form an answer, sometimes in Greek;
and a short conversation between friends, when one
plays on the other a trick which Erasmus played on
More—speaking verses to him as if they were prose.
One Colloquy, the *Poetical Banquet*, seems to be an
account of a real occasion, when Erasmus and his
friends discussed classical texts and false quantities
over a dinner of herbs provided grudgingly by
Erasmus's crabbed housekeeper Margaret, who sends
in beetroot-tops instead of lettuces to see if the poets
will know the difference.

The contemporary abuses passed under review in
the *Colloquies* cover a wide range. Foremost among
them—and this, no doubt, contributed to put the
Colloquies on the Index—are the habits and customs
censured by Luther: the pushing of young people into
monasteries and convents, the exaggerated praise of
celibacy, superstitious reliance on indulgences and
pilgrimages, rash vows, fasting, and the like, and the
doubtful lives of the worst type of monk and friar. It is

noticeable that all this criticism—which rose to a crescendo about 1526—was written and published at a time when Erasmus was publicly disavowing Luther, and insisting on the differences of opinion which separated them. Yet he did not hesitate to add his weight to all the reformer's censures of the superstitions of his time. Erasmus had chosen his standpoint and he never deserted it; he had no intention of parting from the Church of Rome, but he endorsed all efforts to bring about a saner and healthier condition within it.

For this campaign, the dialogue form was a preeminent weapon. It allowed instant penetration of the barbed shaft, with the least ambiguity and circumvention. The dramatic force of the dialogues is tremendous, and they speak for themselves with no need of commentary. They are the voice of the people, as well as the admonition of the scholar from his study.

Why did Erasmus choose a girl, to represent the victim of a type of persuasion which he held in horror, the attempt to stock the monasteries and convents with deluded adolescents? Probably because he wished to show pressure being applied through emotional and imaginative channels on a docile subject, and also because the question was much debated at Bâle, where there was a movement against forcing girls into nunneries, just about the time when the *Colloquies* in question were being written (1523). In that year Erasmus published five new Colloquies dealing with women, and two of them on this subject. It is remarkable how gentle Erasmus was when women or girls were in question, how sympathetically he states their case, treating them entirely as equals with men. In

this he was joining forces with an existing movement among humanists; educated women were to
be found in Renaissance Italy, and whenever the
breath of the Renaissance touched a society, some
women were to be found who flowered into cultivated and intellectual maturity. They were not
always great ladies like Marguerite de Navarre or
Lady Jane Grey; Erasmus had known bourgeois
families where the girls were as highly educated as the
boys, like Pirkheimer's sisters or More's daughters,
and he who had long ago declared that he wished
women to be able to read the Scriptures, now added
the powerful illustration of a gallery of portraits,
collecting together sprightly and subtle and intelligent,
and sometimes learned women.

It is amusing to see Rabelais, influenced by his
admiration for Erasmus and his respect for Marguerite
de Navarre, turning aside occasionally from his rol-
licking stories in which woman is represented frankly
in accordance with the *gaulois* tradition, to repeat
these feminist injunctions of the humanists: "*Que
diray-je? Les femmes et les filles ont aspiré à ceste louange
et manne celeste de bonne doctrine . . .*"

These three Colloquies between a lover and his lass
are designed to combat the idea that celibacy is
necessarily more holy than marriage, as well as to
stigmatise the practice of deceiving young people into
lightly embracing the monastic life. The first, *The
Lover and the Maiden*, is a charming and delicate sketch
of a courtship, in which the arguments put into the
young man's mouth are all in favour of family life,
and a marriage based on compatibility of origins and
temperament. The girl is deliciously quick and subtle

in her teasing vein, and reminds one a little of Rosalind, or the delicate crayon portraits of girls by the Clouets. The other two dialogues, *The virgin averse to marriage* and *The virgin repentant* are more openly propagandist, and Erasmus when writing them must have thought of his own youth, remembering the impression he carried away of the proselytising activities of the Brethren of the Common Life.

Some of the other Colloquies are on the subject of the religious orders and their abuse of power, such as *The Funeral*, with its vivid picture of a deathbed swarming round with greedy and quarrelling monks and friars, contrasted with the quiet, trustful passing of a Christian philosopher free from subservience—one might compare the latter picture with the death of La Boëtie, as described by Montaigne. Superstitious insistence on fasting is the initial topic of the long Colloquy *Ichthyophagia*, with its famous description of the Collège de Montaigu, the most unsavoury recollection of Erasmus's student days. But by far the most celebrated of these Colloquies on the externals of religion are *The Religious Pilgrimage* and *The Shipwreck*. Both rang through Europe, and are still among the best worth reading today, especially *The Shipwreck*, with its vivid and masterly description of a storm at sea. Erasmus hated sea-going, and had experiences of his own in plenty, of crossing the channel in little boats and arriving sick and sorry. This particular story, as related by Adolphus (of Veere) to Antony (of Bergen) is traced by Preserved Smith to the misfortunes of the Scottish merchant ship *Good Fortune*, sailing from Leith to Normandy in January 1516, and driven by storm on the coast of Friesland. It reads like an eye-witness account, from the warning appearance of the St. Elmo's fire, through the various stages of the jettisoning of luggage and the dismemberment of the ship, to the final struggle of the survivors to reach land, clinging to spars in an angry sea. The polemical part of the dialogue is, of course, concerned with the desperate vows and petitions to the saints put up by the passengers in peril of their lives; some vow to become Carthusians, another to go on a pilgrimage to St. James of Compostella barefoot and bareheaded, in a coat of mail and begging his bread all the way, another promises to the figure of St. Christopher on the top of a church in Paris, "rather a mountain than a statue," a wax taper as big as itself. When a more cautious friend reminds the last petitioner that he could never keep his word, he answers in a low voice "lest St. Christopher should hear him"—"You fool, do you think I mean what I say? If I once got safe to shore, I would not give him so much as a tallow candle." This famous incident is one of Erasmus's rare borrowings; it comes from the *Facetiae* of Poggio, an author whom Erasmus usually disliked as obscene, but one who came in opportunely here. And it reappears in Rabelais, where Panurge in his fright during the storm at sea promises a chapel to "Monsieur St. Nicolas," but when the sea is calm again admits that it is all a fiction, *une chapelle d'eau rose*. The robust old priest named Adam who exhorts the passengers in the Colloquy and then plunges half-naked into the sea, has a certain family likeness to Rabelais' Frère Jean.

A good example of Erasmus's modernity of thought can be seen in this Colloquy, where he points out that in antiquity Venus was said to protect sailors, because she was believed to be born of the sea, and the sailors' custom of calling on the Virgin, *stella maris*, was a Christian substitution for the pagan tradition.

The Religious Pilgrimage has a special attraction for English readers, because of its close description of two famous shrines, that of Our Lady of Walsingham and that of St. Thomas at Canterbury. Here Erasmus is drawing entirely from his own recollections, and very clear and vivid they were. He had gone to Walsingham with young Robert Aldridge to act as interpreter, and had even written some Greek verses to hang up in the shrine. But he was not pleased with what he saw. He could not help commenting on the amount of the blessed Virgin's milk which seemed to have been preserved, much as the relics of the true cross would make a ship-load of wood if they were all gathered together; and the transparency of the deceptions practised on every hand on the simple and guileless faithful, are mercilessly revealed. As for the shrine of St. Thomas, the account of the visit there is even more interesting, for he went there with a friend now recognised as no less than John Colet, here called Gratianus Pullus (Pullus = a colt). Under the mighty fabric of the minster, whose great towers welcome pilgrims from afar, they find first the place of Thomas à Becket's martyrdom and the multitude of relics which are brought out, and which they are expected to kiss (Colet draws back and the relics are all shut up again); and then they come to the shrine itself, covered with gold and immense jewels. Here ensues the memorable conversation between Colet and the shower of relics: "Good father," says Colet, "is it true that while he lived, Thomas was very charitable to the poor?" "Very true," says the keeper of the shrine. "And I expect that good inclination in him is not changed, except for the better?" "Undoubtedly." "Then don't you think he would be glad, now that he needs nothing, to relieve the miseries of the poor with all this wealth?" The troublesome visitors are nearly turned out of the cathedral for imagining such a question. Erasmus had had the same thought on looking at the great Chartreuse of Pavia.[1]

The Colloquies on the false trappings of religion are perhaps the most brilliant and the most scathing. But Erasmus had plenty of other bones to pick with his own time. He brings before us a gallery of rogues: the trickster who sells a lame horse and is paid out in his own kind, the "alchemist" who hides the silver in the cinders before discovering it with great triumph in his crucible, the pretended knight who wins respect and a wife through his cheating braggadocio, the soldier of fortune selling his services to the highest bidder and bringing home from the wars poverty, disablement and disease. Two things Erasmus hated with special fervour, as the scourges of his day; war, and the new epidemic which was devastating Europe— syphilis. In his ideas on hygiene he seems to have been in advance of his time; he insisted by instinct on a standard of cleanliness which has only become gener- ally accepted as a result of a greater knowledge of the transmission of disease. Things were tolerated in the

[1] The allusion to the Chartreuse of Pavia is in *The Religious Banquet*; and with it goes a prophetic remark about the shrine of St. Thomas: "I had rather that these superfluities should be applied to charitable uses, than to be reserved for princes that shall one time or other make booty of them."

sixteenth century which shocked him to the core, and one of the most hideous of them is described in *The Marriage that was no Marriage*—the forcible handing over of a beautiful girl to the embraces of a diseased old rake. The danger to the family of the soldier who comes home riddled with venereal disease is plainly spoken of in the dialogue between the soldier and the Carthusian. And Erasmus has general suggestions to make: that barbers should not be surgeons, which was then the universal practice, that no two people should drink out of the same cup, or sleep in the same bed unless they were husband and wife, that inns should give each traveller clean sheets, that the custom of saluting all and sundry with a kiss should be discontinued.

It is in Cervicorn's edition of 1528 that we meet the best of Erasmus's Colloquies on war, and perhaps one of the most artistically perfect in the whole book, *Charon*. In the form of a discussion in the underworld between the ferryman of the "infernal lake" and the Genius Alastor, the messenger, who brings tidings of the state of affairs on earth, it is a comprehensive picture of the turbulent state of Europe and an impartial censure of all sides in the struggle. Erasmus was writing not long after the captivity of Francis I in Madrid as prisoner of the Emperor, at a time when all the nations of Europe appeared likely to fly at each other's throats: "The three monarchs of the world were bent upon each other's destruction with a mortal hatred, and there was no part of Christendom free from the rage of war; for these three have drawn all the rest in to be engaged in the war with them." So Charon is off to buy a new boat which will carry all the ghosts who are coming to him, weighed down by the dreams of the vain things they trusted in on earth, and urged on by the haranguing of the "certain sort of animals in black and white vestments, ash-coloured coats, and various other dresses" who are always hanging about the courts of princes and instilling into them the love of war. According to these people it is a holy war on both sides, for in France they say that: "God is on the French side and they can never be overcome that have God for their protector; in England and Spain the cry is, the war is not the King's but God's."

Two of the Colloquies were written in self-defence: *The Sermon*, a scathing reply to the criticisms of the Franciscan Medardus in a sermon preached in the Cathedral at Augsburg, where he accused Erasmus of presuming to correct the Magnificat and make the blessed Virgin call herself "vile." Erasmus enjoys replying, and corrects the Franciscan's name to a version which would still be appreciated in France (Merdardus). In *Miserly Riches* he replies to accusations of gluttony and insobriety during his stay in Venice: and his defence is perhaps regrettable, since it is based on the most acid description of the parsimony of his host, Andrea da Asola, Aldus's father-in-law. True, it makes amusing reading, and at the end Erasmus admits that different climates require different types of food, but most of his biographers have wriggled uncomfortably when faced with this breach of the etiquette of hospitality. Perhaps he should not have conjured up his picture of the dinner-table in Venice, with seven or eight learned men sitting round a dish where "seven small lettuce leaves swam in vinegar," or faring little better on soup made from boiled cheese, and stale tripe. But Erasmus could not resist a little embroidery, and it was more than twenty years ago.

In two Colloquies Erasmus was perfectly serious: an early one called *The Boy's piety*, written for Erasmius Froben, and the discussion of Christian doctrine entitled *An enquiry concerning Faith* (*Inquisitio de Fide*). The latter holds an important place, for in it one of the speakers (Barbatus) represents Luther, the other (Aulus) an orthodox man such as Erasmus considered himself. It was written before Erasmus had decided to write against Luther, but he never saw reason to disown it; and when at the end Aulus asks: "Well then, since you agree with us (the orthodox) in so many and weighty points, what hinders that you are not wholly on our side?" Barbatus replies, "I have a mind to hear that of you . . ."

But the *Colloquies* would never have enjoyed their lasting fame if they had been merely a weapon of controversy. Even the barbed ones owe their charm less to their incisive attack than to their wit and psychological insight: all are alive, and conjure up pleasant pictures of Renaissance interiors and their inhabitants. A good example of this is the delightful dialogue between the *Abbot and the Learned Lady*, in which the Abbot censures the Lady for the reprehensible habit of leaving classical books lying about everywhere, and she corners him by her skilful arguments in favour of humanistic learning.

The Abbot ends by inviting the Lady to abandon all that nonsense and come to see him at the monastery, when he promises to take her out hunting.

Several of the dialogues on women have no propagandist axe to grind; they reveal an ideal of family life and natural happiness. The friend of the family goes to see the young mother and discusses with her the nurture and education of her son and even the nature of the soul; and long before Rousseau, we find Erasmus issuing a plea to mothers, in the name of Nature, to suckle their own children. The happy wife and the discontented one discuss the proper treatment of husbands, with a wealth of anecdote: one story has been traced to the youth of Thomas More, who married a very young wife and tried to improve her mind, with the result that she threw herself on the floor and wished she was dead. Erasmus must have been present during that first year of marriage, and perhaps saw at first hand how the young husband enlisted his father-in-law to help clear matters up, during a visit to the girl's old home. Another story, of the wife who thoughtfully sent furniture and comforts to the house of her husband's light-of-love, was utilised later on by Marguerite de Navarre (*Heptameron*, Nouvelle XXVIII). In these Colloquies Erasmus speaks as an outsider, but interested in the family life he missed and perhaps regretted. One dialogue only he took from a literary source, the conversation between the young man and the prostitute, where the situation is borrowed from a *comœdia* by the eleventh-century nun Hrotswitha, whose work was discovered and published in 1501. But Erasmus's treatment of the subject is his own, delicate and serious. He was a fastidious person, and his pen was unusually free from coarseness in an extremely outspoken age.

All kinds of scenes and stories are heaped up in

these pages; we are introduced with generous detail
to the neat French inns and the squalid German ones
that he had met on his travels; we hear the four old
men telling their life-histories as they jolt along behind
the waggoner in his cart; we take part in an elaborate
joke played by More and his father-in-law on a superstitious priest, and we see More, like Hamlet, detect-
ing monsters in the clouds; we hear of the polity of
the naked but happy savages in the "new-found
islands," and consider the friendships and antipa-
thies of animals, including the monkey who snuggles
into a corner of the group of the More family painted
by Holbein. Even scientific problems were interesting
Erasmus in his old age (see the Colloquy *On certain
problems*). In these latter instances he was reflecting the
inquiring spirit of his century and generation. But
the noblest positive contribution of the *Colloquies* is in
one of the earliest and in the very last: *The Religious
Banquet* and *The Epicurean*.

In these Colloquies a subject that is familiar to us
from other sources comes to the fore: the *Philosophia
Christi*. The last Colloquy is in its way a *tour de force*,
proving that if virtue is pleasure then the greatest
Epicurean is Christ himself, whose service is perfect
freedom. A fitting end for a book of Erasmus's. But the
Religious Banquet enshrines some of his deepest and
most treasured convictions and ideals. It has often
been observed how much the Renaissance writers
loved picturing friendly talk in a garden: instances are
the setting of the Decameron, or the idyllic resort of
the Florentine philosophers at Careggi. The fact is,
of course, that their minds were penetrated by the
Platonic vision. Erasmus was haunted by it; one of his

earliest extant works, the *Antibarbari*, opened in Platonic style with a description of the speakers sitting under the apple trees, and he wrote no fewer than six Colloquies with the theme of a Banquet or Symposium. The idea of the interweaving of natural beauty and intellectual pleasure, derived from the Platonic dialogues, runs through much of the finest literature of the Renaissance, and gives us not only the exquisite vignettes of Ronsard, losing himself deep in the woods of Vendôme *parlant avec un livre*, but the philosophising of the Forest of Arden and the haunted island of Prospero.

Erasmus's ideal garden is not a magical one, but it breathes nevertheless the true spirit of the Renaissance. It is ordered and stylised, combining shaded walks and little fountains, loggias with symbolic scenes painted on their inner walls, an orchard of rare trees and an aviary, where the philosopher can observe the loves and enmities of the birds. It has its practical side, the cabbage patch and the physic garden, and an open meadow for walking in with company, and beehives, "which is a sight worth seeing," says the contented host; and the little banqueting house at the farthest corner of the meadow is not only a supper-room for the family in summer, but an infirmary in case of infectious diseases. The guests sit down to dine in a summer pavilion, open on three sides to the garden, and after dinner they pass into the library, which also has a gallery looking into the garden and a chapel and study adjoining it.

The conversation over dinner in the garden-room begins on the Bible. It ranges over several topics with the ease of friendship, but the most important is the favourite one of the Christian humanist—the concord between the best in the classical spirit and the spirit of Christ. It is here that the memorable saying comes: *Sancte Socrates, ora pro nobis!* Most of the topics nearest to Erasmus's heart are touched on in this discussion; it is an *Enchiridion* in little, blaming ceremonies and superstitions and vast expense on churches, setting up an ideal of a Christianity founded on right understanding of the words of Christ, and revealing itself in simplicity of heart and charity, intelligent comprehension and serene self-possession. Here, again, is the humanist's religion, much akin to that philosophy of which Montaigne had a vision at the end of his life,[1] *cette vertu suprême, belle, triomphante, amoureuse, délicieuse pareillement et courageuse, ennemie professe et irréconciliable d'aigreur, de desplaisir, de crainte et de contrainte, ayant pour guide nature, fortune et volupté pour compagnes* . . . but with the fundamental difference that Erasmus's philosophy looked beyond the spirit of man for its guide and master, and accepted the doctrine of the redemption of the world.

*   *   *

What is it that marks the *Colloquies* as essentially a work of the Renaissance? It is not the subjects of attack, near as they may be to the ideas of the Reformation, for satire on monks and clergy was common during the Middle Ages, and cheats and liars can be found in any age. It is not the dialogue form, though this is culled from the ancients and beloved by the Renaissance; but something like it had existed before, in drama and in the *jeu-parti*, and in such discussions

[1] *Essais*, chap. xxvi.

as Alain Chartier's *Quadrilogue Invectif*, or in lighter vein, the delicious dialogues of Froissart. It is not the wide sweep of observation, marshalling all sorts and conditions of men, for as we have seen in reference to *The Praise of Folly*, earlier ages loved doing this; there are some strong similarities, for instance, between the *Colloquies* and the Prologue to the *Canterbury Tales*.

A full comparison between the picture of society given by Chaucer and that given by Erasmus has enticing possibilities, but it is outside the scope of this study. To notice a few of the similarities and differences may serve, however, to relate the *Colloquies* to their day and generation. If Erasmus could have known the Prologue—which is unlikely, his command of English being small—he would thoroughly have enjoyed the treatment of the hangers-on of the monastic system: the portraits of the Monk and Friar, the Summoner and Pardoner, would have been entirely after his own heart. For in Chaucer's view of society as well as in Erasmus's, these constitute the defective element. (Curiously enough, where Chaucer draws an endearing portrait of the secular clergy in the "poor Parson of a town," Erasmus's one allusion to them in the Colloquy *Rich Beggars*, is as uncomplimentary as any to the monastic tribe.) The sins of which they are accused are much the same in the two writers, though Chaucer has a genius for physical description which Erasmus lacks, and Erasmus proceeds more through reference to actions committed and words spoken—this is in part due to the choice of the dialogue form. But when we pass to the other members of the party, we are struck by a great difference; in Erasmus's world there is no "parfit gentil

Knight." He is dealing not with the accepted grada-
tion of medieval society, but with a much more fluid
situation; groups are being modified and merging
into each other, money is all-important. If there is any
aristocracy in the *Colloquies*, it is an aristocracy of
intellect, flowering out of a comfortable middle-class
environment like that of the burghers of Bâle.

In Chaucer each portrait is carefully drawn, but
there is little said of the effect on the community of
the individuals named, except in the case of the
Parson and his flock. What marks the *Colloquies* as of
a later age is their strong concentration on social
reform. In fact, Erasmus was in advance of his age in
this. His sense of the debt of each individual to society,
and of the extent to which society holds in its own
hands the key to its improvement, foreshadowed the
eighteenth century. His concern with the ethics of the
individual nearly always relates them to the ethics
of the group, especially when he is concerned with
hygiene, motherhood, or such practical matters. And
yet interacting with his interest in social improvement
is his passionate desire for individual freedom, for
liberty of conscience, which is clogged and fettered
by superstition and custom and traditional subservience. Those two complementary urges, to free and
expand the mental life of the individual, and to
become more and more conscious of his human
environment and its malleability, mark the *Colloquies*
as speaking with the authentic voice of the Renaissance.

Chapter Four

Erasmus on Political Government

IN his satirical works Erasmus was continually aiming at the transformation and improvement of the society he observed. It was mainly by the dissolving agent of ridicule that he tried to eliminate the useless or harmful conventions of his time, and his irony was a powerful weapon of destruction. There are, however, throughout his work, and even in the most biting of his satires, positive suggestions and constructive plans, and out of the whole emerges an ideal of the state, general in outline but including many practical ideas specifically applied to contemporary conditions. Erasmus's immense output of religious and secular writings, prefaces, letters, commentaries, essays, dialogues, treatises, are wonderfully homogeneous. He repeated himself almost as much as Voltaire, but he contradicted himself remarkably little, and each successive addition to the *Opera Erasmi* corroborated and amplified a personal outlook, and added details to his particular vision of the good life.

In turning his mind to social problems he was, as we have seen, essentially a man of his age. Other writers of the Renaissance were engaged in a similar attempt to reform existing conditions or to put forward methods of social organisation. There are two books in particular which invite comparison with

Erasmus's ideas: the *Utopia* of Thomas More and Machiavelli's *Prince*. The *Utopia* indeed, contained a great deal of Erasmian thought; it was rumoured that Erasmus was the author of the first part of the book, and though he had to deny the allegation, it was by no means so embarrassing as some rumours of the kind. He and More were so closely linked by thought and temperament, that the interpenetration of their ideas is a matter of course. But the *Utopia*, for all its presentation of serious theories, has an element of fantasy and proposes itself as an ideal quite distinct from any reality in the Europe of its day: the city where all goods are in common, where gold is useless except as a pretty toy for the children, and where the citizen must ask leave of his father and his wife before he can go for a walk in the country, is a fable as well as a storehouse of immortal and fruitful ideas. Erasmus's views on government are of a humbler and less radical kind; they have strict reference to the actual conditions he wanted to improve, they accept certain conventions and utilise certain existing methods; they represent neither a completely new hypothesis like More's, nor a series of purely practical reforms like Voltaire's, touching the surface only and leaving the principles unchanged. It is as if the two friends, (Erasmus and More) had pooled their ideas during those years culminating in 1516. In that year both their treatises on government were finished: Erasmus's *Education of a Christian Prince* was printed by June 17th, and More sent Erasmus a manuscript copy of the *Utopia* on September 3rd. There is no doubt that they had shared their opinions and interchanged ideas in discussion for a long time past; and the result was that the substratum remained the same, though the more daring and inventive genius of More produced a classic which stands out as applicable to any age, and the reflective but practical nature of Erasmus produced a more modest treatise specially applied to the needs of his own time.

And Machiavelli? Erasmus probably never read the *Prince*, as although written in 1513, it was published much later (1536): and it would no doubt have shocked him profoundly. But Machiavelli was writing for a society in process of disintegration, his chief design being to show how the political instability of the Italian states could be arrested—by a clever and unscrupulous despot. Erasmus had behind him the sturdy and solid self-respect of the towns of the Netherlands, and under his eyes the free institutions of the Swiss cantons: no wonder that freedom is an essential idea in his view of government. Machiavelli wrote from a deeply pessimistic standpoint, the profound wickedness of human nature being a necessary assumption in his scheme. Erasmus's hopes for the future depend entirely upon the teachableness of man, especially of the destined ruler, and his view of human nature is realistic, admitting both good and evil in man's make-up, but estimating as more important the element of good.

There are clear and inevitable contrasts between many of Erasmus's political ideas and the corresponding ones in Machiavelli, and the general contrast between the Machiavellian despot and the Erasmian prince is too black-and-white to admit of emphasis. But some essential principles they share. To Erasmus, as to Machiavelli (and for that matter, to Montesquieu) the safest government, in good conditions, was neither monarchy, aristocracy nor democracy, but a mixed type. And if it is true that Machiavelli especially typifies the belief of his age that all bodies tend perpetually towards disintegration and can only be held together by continued vigilance and effort, the same is implied in Erasmus's suggestions for political organisation. To him also the Golden Age was in the past, and improvement was not a matter of progress but of harking back to the precepts and practice of a wiser generation. Above all, he recognised with the other writers of his time that government was about to be vested more seriously than ever in the single person of a prince. This Erasmus possibly regretted, and he certainly preferred an elective to a hereditary monarchy; but in proposing ways by which the single ruler could be educated so as to become the protector and representative of the people, he was accommodating himself to the circumstances of the age and facing facts as they really were.

His social and political ideas are to be found scattered throughout his writings. A number are in the long comments added to the *Adagia* in Froben's edition of 1515, and in later editions; and some of the essays contained there had a separate life of their own like the *Dulce bellum inexpertis*, reprinted separately several times. The *Moria* and the *Colloquies* teem with ideas on social reform; even the commentaries on the New Testament have their share, and the Letters re-echo the humanist's prevailing meditations, often severely critical. But the chief period of his political activity as a writer, and his attempts to intervene in current affairs, begins in 1516, when he entered upon his duties as a councillor of Charles of Burgundy, later Charles V, and wrote for him the *Education of a Christian Prince* (1516) and the *Complaint of Peace* (1517). At this time his own success and confidence were at their height, and the chances of peace in Europe seemed brighter than they were ever to be again in the rest of Erasmus's lifetime. By 1523, it was becoming clear that reasoned argument could do nothing to divert the stream of events, and Erasmus, who had addressed the Prefaces of his *Paraphrases* to one Prince after another in the hope of stemming the tide, became a spectator once more.

He was not a specialist with experience of state-craft. That is one of the great differences between the Erasmian view and those of More or Machiavelli, both of whom were actively engaged in the business of government. Erasmus was an amateur at the game, writing from the quiet of his study in the city over-looking the Rhine; he was not personally responsible for the conduct of a country's affairs. Yet this aspect of the case must not be over-emphasised either: Erasmus's study, far from being a backwater, was the meeting-place of all the currents of thought in Europe. He had certainly a larger circle of acquaintance than any other writer of his time, perhaps of almost any time: "no one but Voltaire met as many and as different kinds of men."[1] His vast correspondence witnesses to this. The people who figure in it are of all types and conditions, ranging from noblemen and officials high at Court, University professors and theologians, Bishops and Cardinals, to bankers,

[1] Renaudet. *Études érasmiennes*, p. 65. I am much indebted to this book, both for the present chapter and the final one.

merchants, city officials, schoolmasters, doctors, students—a good cross-section of the middle class of his time. As well as these he had actually known some of the great, who were engaged in political activity, Popes, Kings and Princes, such as Leo X, Henry VIII and several princes of the Empire, and the Emperor himself, for whom he wrote the *Education of a Christian Prince*. All these contacts kept him posted with the latest news of Europe, and this constitutes one of his claims to originality: he was the man of his century who could best survey the whole European scene. In the first flood of the spirit of nationalism, one person was watching the *entrechoc* of nations with a lucid and penetrating eye, and deriving from the prospect the first true idea of international relations on a general scale: and that man was Erasmus.

He wrote not as a politician, but as a moralist. This perhaps accounts for the fact that his views on government have been to a certain extent ignored by writers on political theory; it is only in recent years that students have turned to Erasmus and discovered in his writings the germ of many of the ideas which become fruitful in later generations. For the purposes of this study, we may have two objects in view in considering briefly what those views were. One will be to show how they also illustrate the Erasmian compromise, a delicate balance between extremes, and between ideal and reality: the other, to see how in their genesis and development, these opinions illustrate exactly the process of thought characteristic of the Renaissance.

*　　*　　*

It was inevitable that the state envisaged by Erasmus should be a monarchy. Not only did his friends and advisers in the classical world, from Plato and Aristotle to Cicero and Plutarch, accept monarchy as the best form of government, but the practical necessities of his own day called for that approach; a large part of Erasmus's specific writing on statecraft is addressed personally to one or other of the reigning princes of his time. He did not accept the principle of kingship without reserve. It is only very cautiously that he admits the merits of the rule of one; he explicitly held with Plato that where monarchy is the best type of state, tyranny is the worst, and for the one not to degenerate into the other, the monarch must be hedged round not by divinity but by more tangible safeguards. Erasmus had a double line of despots ever before his eyes: the tyrants of the past—Claudius, Caligula, Nero—and the rulers of his own day whose ambitions plunged their people into war, misery and distress. Not for nothing had he watched the trials of his native Netherlands after the fiery rule of Charles the Bold, and the miseries brought to France by the moonstruck dreams of Charles VIII, who was fired by his boyhood's reading of the romances of the Round Table, and imagined that by invading Italy he was proving himself another of the paladins.

Erasmus's picture of the ideal prince owes much to the past. It is a composite picture, drawn partly from antiquity, partly from the Bible and partly from the needs of the modern age. These three strands are interwoven throughout Erasmus's dealings with matters of state. In agreement with antiquity are his ideas about the person of the prince, the importance of his education and upbringing, the view that no state will be truly happy until its king is a philosopher or its philosophers rule. So said Plato, and it is to Plato above all that Erasmus is indebted. He agreed that the ideal prince preserves truth above all things, is temperate, wise, just, cautious, but also possessing the ability to act. He must have an active brain, a good memory, and careful training; he must also be able to endure physical strain and to watch while his people sleep. He is not the slave of his own passions: that is the character of the tyrant. He is self-controlled, his personal life is modest and not luxurious, his desires and pleasures are mental rather than sensual. Above all, he is the father of his people. All his relations with them are based on this analogy: he will be slow to punish and seek revenge, quick to protect and untiring in his watchfulness and activity for the good of the common people.

From many sources Erasmus culled the analogy between the state and the human body, the king being the head or the mind. It is found in Cicero, one of Erasmus's favourite writers. Other pagan writers saw in the prince the image of God, the shepherd of his people, the pilot of the ship of state; they drew contrasting portraits of the true king and the tyrant, emphasising the servitude of the latter to his favourites and the fear with which his life was surrounded. After Plato, Erasmus perhaps drew most upon the writings of Plutarch, Cicero and Seneca, and in this he was setting an example for the whole of the sixteenth century.

Princeps imago Dei: how much more forcefully this

theme can be expanded in Christian times! The prince will be taught early to know the Scriptures and to model himself upon the precepts of Christ. He will be familiar at an early age with the New Testament, and even before that he will have read *Proverbs*, *Ecclesiastes*, the *Book of Wisdom*, all the legacy of a great king. In his reading of classical history he will remember that he is recalling the deeds of pagans, and he, a Christian, is called upon to surpass them in virtue. In the ascetic principles proposed to the young prince, there is a harmony between the stoicism of Seneca and the teaching of the Gospel which exactly fulfils Erasmus's ideas. But the Christianity to which he calls his prince is by no means an empty name, and it contains austerities which surpass the require-ments of the classical philosophers. "You, too, must take up your cross, or else Christ will have none of you. What can be my cross? you ask. I will tell you. Follow the right, do violence to no one, plunder no one, sell no public office, be corrupted by no bribes. While you are using every means and interest to benefit the state, your life is fraught with care; you rob your youth and spirits of pleasure, you wear your-self down with long hours of toil; forget all that and take your pleasure in the satisfaction of a good con-science. Your private emotions as a man, revengeful anger, love for your wife, hatred of an enemy, or shame, will urge you to do what is not right, and what is to the detriment of the common weal; let the thought of honour win, let the good of the state entirely con-quer your personal feelings. If you cannot defend your kingdom without violating justice, shedding much blood and injuring the cause of religion, give up your crown and yield to the necessities of the times. If you cannot protect the affairs of your subjects except at the peril of your own life, set the safety of the people before your very life! While you are acting thus, like a truly Christian prince, there will be some who call you a dolt, and no prince at all. Be steadfast in mind, prefer rather to be a just man than an unjust prince. You see now, I think, that even the greatest kings are not without their cross, if they wish to follow the right at all times, as they should."

The young prince, then, in the *Institutio Principis Christiani*, is first formed as to character: it is the love of virtue which is the first aim of his tutor's teaching. Then comes the acquiring of wisdom. As the first has been the province of the Bible, the second is that of secular reading, which to Erasmus means the classics. Here he recommends Plutarch, then Seneca, Aristotle and Cicero, but above all Plato; and also the historians, who like the historical books of the Bible, should be read with the greatest caution, referring everything to a Christian standard. We do not want our young princes modelling themselves on Achilles or Alexander (still less on Arthur and Lancelot!). After the moral and the intellectual education, comes a more technical training; he is to learn to know his own kingdom, to study its geography and history, its provinces and cities with their laws, customs, institutions and so on. He is to go to see its different parts, so as to understand them and to win the love of his subjects (for this it is better that the prince should be born and brought up among the people whom he is to rule).

The Bible, the classics, the experience of things

themselves—it is not hard to recognise in this the typical education of the Renaissance, where touched with the breath of Reform. Rabelais, in some famous chapters of the *Gargantua* (XXIII–IV) sketched at length a very similar programme, though on gigantic lines.

All this discussion of the education of the prince is contained in the first chapter of the treatise, and suggests that to Erasmus the greatest safeguard that could be applied to the institution of monarchy is the insistence on the good character of the prince. Here Erasmus is speaking for his optimistic generation, with their faith in the transforming power of education and the magic of knowledge. But there are other safeguards, and we find that Erasmus's prince will never be a despot, however enlightened; an absolute monarchy might be the best thing if a perfect ruler were to be found, but as this is impossible, what we call a constitutional monarchy is the safest. "If an average prince (as the affairs of men go now) is to be found, it will be better to have a limited monarchy checked and lessened by aristocracy and democracy. Then there is no chance for tyranny to creep in, but just as the elements in nature balance each other, so will the state hold together under similar control." If the prince is good, his power will not be lessened by these controls, but if he is bad, the state will not be at the mercy of a single man.[1]

The important thing is that the prince should remember that he is the servant of his people. His whole

---

[1] In the *Lingua* (1525) Erasmus describes an ideal monarchy, where the power of the sovereign is tempered by synods, urban councils and public consent.

life is dedicated to their service, and his interests are always to cede to theirs. Man is free, says Erasmus, and free twice over: he is born free, and Christ came to give us liberty. The Christian prince rules, therefore, over a free people, and should be as far as possible from the tyrant, who can only keep his throne by crushing the spirit out of his subjects, impoverishing them and setting them at each other's throats. All his edicts are directed to his own preservation, all those of the king to the preservation of the state.

It may well be that when Erasmus drew his picture and laid such stress on the freedom of the people and on the value of self-identification of the king with the people (especially when he makes the point that the king should be born and brought up in his own dominions), he was thinking specifically of Charles himself and of the Duchy of Burgundy. Erasmus himself was a subject of that realm, having been born in Holland, and though his international situation and outlook, and the fact that he chose to live so little in his own country, have obscured the fact of his being "Roterodamus," some critics of his work see in his political ideas a strong connection with the sturdy independence of the Netherlands and their sense of unification under Burgundy. It is very probable that the atmosphere of his youth had something to do with the formation of his attitude to kingship, just as it had with the fundamental principles of the *Philosophia Christi.*

At all events, he spoke a warning to the future Charles V when he advocated a close understanding between the people and their native-born ruler, and deprecated the idea of a universal monarchy. The young prince to whom he spoke, born at Ghent, was in a position to fulfil his requirements with regard to the possessions of Burgundy, but he was soon to become Emperor of a wider domain than any ruler had held since the Roman Empire, and all the ills Erasmus most feared for the public must ensue.

It will be seen that the *Institutio* is a compromise between an ideal and a set of practical suggestions. The recommendation of a limited monarchy is in itself an example of Erasmian compromise. In spite of Erasmus's vindication of the people's freedom and the care for their welfare which many of his reforms suggest, he is far from extolling them or echoing *vox populi, vox Dei*. The people are to be free, but they are to be ruled, and by a prince who has been able through a judicious education to shake off the false ideas which the common people widely accept. The humanist's views on the proletariat of his day are a curious mixture of protectiveness and contempt. Yet it is to be noticed that the relation between prince and people, as Erasmus sees it, is a mutual understanding for the good of both parties, and resembles a tacit contract. In this he was foreshadowing the most important works of later political science.

It is in the details of his plan for state reform that Erasmus seems modern. These details are mainly given in the latter chapters of the *Education of a Christian Prince*, which deal with the arts of peace, with finance and law, but they may be amplified from other sources such as the *Colloquies*.

Law, under the true prince, is based on equity and not directed either to the profit of the crown or to gain for any class, but it looks solely to the welfare of the people as a whole. The prince himself is a kind of living law, and he will take care to frame a few just laws rather than to pile up decrees. A very few laws will suffice for a well-organised state under a good prince and trustworthy officials. The buying and selling of public offices ought not to be tolerated, and although the common people should not be encouraged to discuss the laws, the prince should take care to make laws that are pleasing to all good citizens. Penal laws have as their object the deterring of people from crime, but the prevention of crime goes much further back than that, and the prince, like the good physician, should attempt to diagnose the causes of evil and remove them, rather than depend on punishments for eradicating crime. For every reason he will encourage education. Here Erasmus goes further than most of his contemporaries, in recommending universal education, for both boys and girls (here he was perhaps remembering Plato). This is the most essential thing of all; the spread of good principles would be more efficacious than anything in ridding a state of crime. Another essential part in the prevention of crime is the suppression of the idle classes, especially the beggars, itinerant monks, street pedlars, and other social parasites with which Erasmus's age abounded. He classes with them money-lenders and brokers, gamekeepers, and the host of idle retainers kept for show in the service of the rich, and he suggests that limitation of the number of monasteries might be a good thing, as in some cases the monastic life led merely to a sluggish ease. (Of course, genuine cases of sickness or destitute old age must be cared for in public

136

institutions for the purpose.) Erasmus is radical about idleness. He condemns the "busy time-wasting" of the soldier's life, and he cannot see why the title of nobility should ever grace a life of indolence. Let the well-born keep their honours if they excel in true nobility, as their fathers who won those titles did. But why should an idle person with no other claim to notice than charming manners and a taste for gambling be placed on a higher level than the shoemaker or the farmer? The greatest claim to honour is usefulness to one's fellow-men. Like Voltaire, Erasmus recommends old families or wealthy citizens to teach a useful profession to their sons.

Erasmus gives several examples of laws which have degenerated into injustice, such as the heaping up of customs duties, the confiscation of goods after a ship-wreck, the taking over by the Crown of the goods of a foreigner who dies out of his own country. All those practices were first established as a matter of protec-tion for the rightful owners or heirs, but have been corrupted into a new form of theft. And the worst corruption of the idea of law happens when the ruler applies it for his own purposes alone, punishing the loss of a penny from the royal treasury more severely than theft which reduces a poor man to beggary, or wielding a tyrannical vengeance upon the accusation of *lèse-majesté*.

It is in his remarks about finance that Erasmus comes down to close details. Like his contemporaries and successors, he conceives of only a controlled economy. The state he portrays is not a communal one as in *Utopia*, but one in which the law regulates the production and distribution of wealth. Erasmus dislikes disproportionate riches; the power of money in the hands of a few, more marked in his day than ever before, seemed to him a power for evil. He suggests control by the state, sumptuary laws to prevent waste and display, heavy taxation of luxuries and lightening of taxation on essential goods such as bread, beer, wine, clothing. Especially he insists that monopolies and tax-farming should not exist in a well-ordered state. The common people are to be relieved of their burdens, the workers on the land are especially to be favoured, and the anomalies and injustices of feudal taxation are to be reformed. The public money is to be spent on productive ends, on building and adorning cities, draining swamps, bringing waste land to cultivation, and the prince is to see that the land is used for the purpose to which it is suited.

Faced with the rise of capitalism, Erasmus as usual takes a middle way. Some of its forms he tolerates or approves, such as banking, and the establishment of great commercial houses like the firms of Fugger or Froben. Some forms of capitalistic enterprise he thoroughly condemns, especially speculation and money-lending; to see priests involved in usury is horrifying to him. He is suspicious about other forms of enterprise because he fears they mask some less reputable activity—colonisation, for instance, may be a form of pillage (and thus the clear-sighted Erasmus of the *Colloquies* has his word to say on the age of discovery). All forms of profiteering by the rise in prices come under his condemnation, and he is not sure about the ethics of free competition in every kind of trade, though as a whole he approves of it,

138

but not of the piling up of wealth which results. In bookselling, for instance, he would rather see control exercised by the trade, as in the older crafts by the city guilds. In fact, he wants a modified system in which the state controls the distribution of money, and he regrets the fading out of local controls, exercised of old by the cities themselves, who regulated prices, weights and measures, and quality of goods.

It is curious to see how many of these fiscal and social reforms are identical with those suggested by Voltaire, and to reflect how their adoption in the age of Erasmus would possibly have avoided many later tragedies, including the French Revolution. And yet often Erasmus was looking backward rather than forward when he proposed them; many of his remedies are prompted by a nostalgic recollection of the older urban economy of the towns of the Netherlands, which imposed a communal control on industry and kept prices down and value up. The warnings about feudal taxation, an idle aristocracy and the abuse of tax-farming are, however, very much akin to the *Lettres Philosophiques* or the *Lettres Persanes*.

Above all, if a kingdom is to be administered rightly, there is one essential condition: peace. The *Education of a Christian Prince* has little to say about so negative a thing as war, until the last chapter, which summarises the reasons for refusing to engage in war until the very last extremity. Erasmus will admit war in self-defence, but for no other cause, and he can hardly bring himself to consider that any war at all could be called "just." War is formally banned by Christ. And the ruin war brings with it, the loss in life and happiness, the collapse of prosperity, the decline in morality, the cost of destruction, so much exceeding the cost of peaceful living—surely no war can be worth all these, and certainly not the kind of war Erasmus witnessed. To a modern historian Erasmus would seem to be confusing the superficial and the fundamental causes of war, when he dwells on the pretexts offered by the hasty actions of young princes— a broken treaty, a fiancée accepted into the family of her future husband and then rejected for political reasons (like the little Margaret of Austria, brought to France at the age of two as the future queen of Charles VIII, but sent back eleven years later when Charles saw the chance of marrying Anne of Brittany).[1] But in emphasising the responsibility of the prince in these matters, Erasmus is fulfilling what he considers to be his duty to his own sovereign: he was after all writing for the eye of a prince.

He became less and less favourably inclined to the institution of monarchy, as he watched the way in which the princes of his day were managing between them to wreck the prospects of Europe. Everything Erasmus held most dear depended for its existence upon peace, and no topic aroused so passionate a defence under his pen. As one of his early translators said of the *Complaint of Peace*, "perceiving and feeling the world to be wavering, troublesome, unquiet, and everywhere bent and inclined to war and mischief, he could not temper himself nor yet his pen; but needs he must write unto the world this true and eloquent

[1] Erasmus has a word of pity for those unfortunate girls who lose home and friends as they are moved about like pawns in the political game.

complaint . . ."[1] Long before the *Complaint of Peace* he had written on this subject; as early as 1504, in the Panegyric he was commissioned to write for Philip of Burgundy, he had associated the ideal of the prince with the duty of peacemaking; in Italy he had written an *Antipolemus* against the warlike activities of Julius II, which is now lost, though it is perhaps reflected in the fierce satire of the dialogue *Julius Exclusus* (whether or not this is Erasmus's work, editors have failed to decide). The *Adagia* were full of allusions to war, and the essay on *Dulce bellum inexpertis* ("War is sweet to those who know it not") ran into several separate editions. Prefaces were used for the same purpose, especially the preface to the new edition of the *Enchiridion* in 1518, and letters to the princes of his time, e.g. to Leo X, to Francis I, offered scope for the expansion of Erasmus's ideas. The most complete effort that he made in this cause remains the *Complaint of Peace*.

It is when he writes on war and peace that Erasmus seems nearest to our own time. All that he says on this subject strikes a modern note, his arguments are still valid, his proposals have barely begun to be applied. His horror of war was both a deep personal emotion and the outcome of his study of Christian doctrine; and his arguments are based partly on rational grounds—the ruin and devastation of war, the fact that man alone in all nature is self-destructive—and on the clear leading of Christ, whose service entails an attitude towards others which is the very antithesis of war. It is impossible to follow Christ and prosecute

[1] Tr. Thomas Paynell. Reprinted with introduction by W. J. Hutten, New York, 1946.

a war for gain such as Erasmus saw going on round him, and indeed he doubts very much whether there can be any "just" war at all. War is not made by the people, in Erasmus's view, therefore it is always an attack on their freedom. It is inevitably the work of a few, and those are the leaders of men, who should be their safeguards. Erasmus diagnoses the causes of war, some of which are applicable particularly to his own day; others, acutely observed, are perennial.

First, there are disputes on succession to the throne, marriage alliances and hereditary rights, the curse of his century and the next. Secondly, there are private causes of quarrelling among princes, injuries resented, imaginary or otherwise, personal relations of various kinds. Thirdly, there is the blind convention of national feeling: the Englishman and the Frenchman hate each other, the German, the Scot, the Spaniard, have their customary quarrels, and yet no national boundary separates one Christian from another. But there are other, more sinister, causes of war, and here Erasmus's clear-sightedness stands him in good stead. He points out that the tyrant is only enabled to remain in power as long as his people are weak, and his interest is to keep them so. For this purpose he will not only take obvious opportunities to involve them in war; he will send out agitators to stir up ill feeling and create war between nations, simply for the purpose of preserving the power of the despot. Erasmus was fully awake to the possibilities of preparing a campaign by a stream of propaganda.

Furthermore, there are certain classes of people who only flourish in war: in peace they are out of a job.

All the efforts of these individuals will be directed towards producing a state of affairs in which they can squeeze power and profit out of the common ruin.

Finally, Erasmus declared that in his own day the cause of war was most served by those very people who by their profession should be attempting to quench it: the servants of the Church herself, religious advisers to monarchs, popular preachers, ecclesiastical dignitaries who should be advising toleration and pointing to the love of Christ for all mankind and the fatherhood of God. Instead of this, they are inciting kings to battle and their congregations to nationalistic hatred and longing for war.

What can be done in a practical way to diminish the chance of war? Erasmus has several concrete proposals to make. In the first place, work to modify nationalistic feeling, encourage understanding between peoples, make it clear that war between Christians, of whatever nationality, is civil war, and cannot be in a just cause. Secondly, stabilise the frontiers of Europe, and let each sovereign be content with what has fallen to his lot. Thirdly, let the order of succession be uniform and recognised, so that no deadly quarrels can arise from that. Fourthly, make it impossible for a prince to declare war of his own accord: war is so serious that only the whole people have the right to take such a step. Fifthly, organise arbitration. Are there not bishops, abbots, nobles, of wisdom and experience, councils and senates, serious bodies of men who could be called upon to mediate between parties? Sixthly, mobilise all the moral forces of the world against the idea of war; education, Christian idealism, the authority of the Church, public opinion.

In these ways a real effort may be made to rid the world of the scourge.

Never was Erasmus in deadlier earnest than when he discussed the preservation of peace. Peace was a necessary condition of all he valued in life—the evangelising of the world, the spread of Good Learning, the victory of intellectual and spiritual values. He saw the state of affairs so clearly that his words apply equally well to war as it was in his day or to war as it might become. He saw the truth behind the claptrap and recognised the increasing use of artillery for the menace that it was.[1] Perhaps his dislike of the Arthurian romances has its roots in this: in an age which tried to preserve or resurrect the glamour of the medieval tourney, and only succeeded in producing empty copies of a spectacle which had lost its *raison d'être* by the dying of chivalry, Erasmus despised and hated anything which helped to blind people to the terrible reality. Less and less would the rules of knighthood apply to the unscrupulous business of modern war, and the sooner the gilding was removed to let the truth appear in its stark brutality, the better. Erasmus makes a curious counterpart to Don Quixote.

The *Complaint of Peace* ends with an impassioned climax, often quoted, and worth quoting again. It is an appeal to high and low, to the whole body of Christian people, and through it the word *Appello*

[1] "Whose invention was a cannon? Was it not the invention of the meek, lowly, merciful followers of Jesus Christ, whose law was love, and whose last legacy to his disciples and the world, peace?" Erasmus mentions the custom of giving pieces of cannon the names of the apostles: "Paul, the constant teacher and preacher of peace, gives a name to a piece of artillery, and is thus made to hurl a deadly ball at the head of a Christian! The Church militant with a vengeance!"

rings like Zola's *J'accuse*. "I appeal to you, Princes, on whose nod human affairs depend, you who stand for the image of Christ among men; acknowledge the voice of your King calling you to peace, realise that the whole world, wearied by continuous calamities, beseeches you for peace. Whatever cause of complaint one of you may have, let him sacrifice it to the common happiness: this matter is too grave for small things to stand in its way. I appeal to you, Priests, consecrated to God, to use all your strength in spreading abroad that which you know to be most agreeable to God, and in repelling what you know God hates. I appeal to you, Theologians, preach the Gospel of peace, let it resound continually in the ears of the people. I appeal to you, Bishops, I appeal to you, nobles and magistrates, I appeal to all of you everywhere who call yourselves Christians, to unite together with one heart and mind, and show how much can be done against the power of tyrants by the union of the whole people. Let eternal peace join together those who are united in so many ways by nature, and still more by Christ." Everything pleads in favour of peace, nature, humanity, Christ Himself; and the appeal ends in a somewhat pathetic attempt to associate with these profound forces, the figures moving on the stage of the Renaissance world: Pope Leo, *pacificus ille placidusque*, Francis I, who does not disdain to pray for peace, Prince Charles, that youth of uncorrupted mind, the Emperor Maximilian and the noble King Henry of England.

On these and on their advisers depends for Erasmus the fate of his own time, and during the next few years he took his own advice and did his best to influence them. If the peaceful intervention of a man of letters was ever to have any weight, it might well have been at that moment and proceeding from that pen, whose prestige was so international and so marked. For the purpose he chose his *Paraphrases* on the New Testament, a new form of commentary which was likely to be widely read (they were in fact, so much appreciated that an Injunction of Edward VI later recommended that a copy be kept in every parish church in England). The case was desperate; war was on the point of breaking out between Francis I and the Emperor, and had indeed begun in the Low Countries by the time Erasmus was ready to address to Charles (now Charles V) his preface to the Paraphrase of St. Matthew (January 1522). He wrote to others in that year (to Prince George of Saxony in May, in the Preface to the *Treatise on Letter-Writing*, and to the new Pope Adrian VI in September in the Preface to *Arnobius on the Psalms*), denouncing the rivalry of the French King and the Emperor and pleading the cause of peace. The next Paraphrase, on St. John, he addressed to the Emperor's brother, Archduke Ferdinand, in January 1523, and in December it was the turn of Francis I with the Paraphrase of St. Mark. In the meantime Adrian VI had died— the scholarly Fleming with whom Erasmus might have had much in common—and a new Pope, Clement VII, received the Paraphrase on the Acts of the Apostles, in January 1524. "Thus, through the medium of the Gospel and by the will of the prince of the Renaissance, was realised, in a purely theoretical but moving way, the first league of nations."[1]

[1] P. Mesnard, *L'essor de la Philosophie politique*, p. 116.

The frail hope soon failed. As well try to dam a flood by reasoning with it! The war went on, and in 1524 Henry VIII invaded France to attack the Somme towns as an ally of the Emperor. Erasmus's attempts at intervention were over, and he returned to the rôle of the spectator, avid of news and keenly interested in events. He hoped that the resounding victory of the Emperor over Francis I at Pavia would at last bring the war to an end, and the treaty of Madrid become an instrument of peace. But no sooner had Francis got home from his captivity in Madrid, than the terms of the treaty were repudiated by France and the struggle continued. Erasmus watched, remembering, no doubt, that he had written that the evil prince is the instrument of God's chastisement of his people. He appeared unmoved even by the terrible news of the sack of Rome by the troops of the Emperor in 1527, but the extent of his disappointment can be seen in the Colloquy *Charon* (1528).

ALASTOR: All that fame has told you is very true: for I myself, having been a constant companion of the Furies, have with these eyes seen more than all this, and that they never at any time have proved themselves more worthy of their name than now.

CHARON: But there is danger lest some good spirit should start up and of a sudden exhort them to peace. And men's minds are variable, for I have heard that among the living there is one Polygraphus, who is continually, by his writing, inveighing against wars, and exhorting to peace.

ALASTOR: Ay, ay, but he has a long time been talking to the deaf. . . .

*   *   *

A critic of Erasmus's political ideas says that he was by theory a democrat, by temperament an aristocrat, by force of circumstances a monarchist. This pleasant epigram is subject to caution, as nowhere does Erasmus counsel any form of government but a monarchy; he consistently advocates the form of limited monarchy in which the sovereign is controlled by other powerful elements in the state. Nowhere does he give any detailed suggestion of how this is to be achieved; the idea of the representation of the people is not explicitly to be found in his works, although the "local councils and public consent" which he mentions in the *Lingua* indicates some form of elective representation, and the referendum. But the epigram is true in essence, for Erasmus only accepted Monarchy as a practical measure; he could put up with kings when they were there, though he would rather see them elective than hereditary; but all his respect goes to an aristocracy of education and intellect, all his pity to the common people. He does not credit the people with the wisdom to govern themselves; but he sees government as entirely directed to their good, to the preservation of their rights and their prosperity, as in fact delegated by the people to the reigning monarch, who governs in their name. He is as far as possible from the theory of the divine right of kings.

The process by which Erasmus reached his views on government, as illustrated by the *Education of a Christian Prince*, is a process of thought typical of the Renaissance. Principles culled from a wide reading of the classics, principally from Plato, are set for comparison beside the teaching of Christ, which infuses

148

into them a higher spiritual significance: the intellectual maturity of the classics mingles with the spiritual maturity of the Gospels. To the theories thus obtained is added the experience of men and affairs, the observation of modern problems and needs and dangers. Out of it all comes a composite series of practical suggestions that are new in their implications, if old in their origins: the idea of the contract between prince and people; the idea of universal education without discrimination of class or sex, and backed up by freedom of opinion and of the press; the abolishing of the practice of buying offices of state; the reform of taxation on a rational basis; the restriction of wealth; the proposal for settlement by arbitration in the face of a threat of war—all these suggestions show how fruitful, in such a mind as Erasmus's, was the conjunction he so earnestly sought, between antiquity, the Gospel, and the lessons of experience.

Chapter Five

The Lutheran Tragedy

"TRAGEDY" was the term consistently applied by Erasmus to the first beginnings of what we, looking back, call the Reformation. He saw the first twenty years of that cleavage, which developed to so much greater proportions after he was gone, and he deprecated it from first to last, blaming equally Luther and Luther's enemies for the violence with which the whole affair was handled. To him it was "these odious dissensions," "this stupid and pernicious tragedy," though at the news of Luther's marriage he added with a wry smile, "perhaps one should call it a comedy, since it ends with wedding bells."

More has been written about this aspect of Erasmus's life than about any other, and with reason. The impact of the violent character of Luther on the humanist's world, the gradual change of Erasmus's attitude as he watches the development of Luther's career, the clash between them, and the solitary position persistently adopted by Erasmus, are not only interesting in themselves—they are profoundly symbolic. Behind them lie great fields of controversy: the long history of medieval philosophy, branching away from Augustine into a theory and practice which disgusted Luther and drove him into his extreme reaction against it and back towards Augustine; and the great discussion at the root of humanism, as to how

150

far human efforts and mortal visions are of value in themselves, and how far ethics and the love of beauty can go to save a human soul. Above all, the clash is one of character: it provides a psychological study, in which the two minds so strongly contrasted seem to stand for two essentially different types of humanity, two different aspects of the longing of mankind for its highest good. There is no easy answer to the conundrums it raises, and doubtless no one will ever be able to unravel the convolutions it produced in Erasmus's subtle and sensitive mind. It was easy for his contemporaries and critics to call him vacillating and timid, but when his conduct is looked at with an impartial eye, it is not that of a coward: it is rather that of a man whose thoughts and desires are on so different a plane from those of his adversaries that there must needs be perpetual misunderstanding between them. If Erasmus had been a coward, he could easily have curried favour with the Pope, damned Luther from the beginning, and accepted a fat bishopric. But was he who had preached concord to join in the howls of Luther's enemies and condemn him unheard? "Far be such a thought from the mind of Erasmus." When he finally wrote against Luther, it was on a philosophical topic, keeping the controversy in the realms of the intellect, and still intending to convince rather than to suppress the reformer.

Again, it is easy to do as some modern critics have done, and erect in place of Erasmus and Luther two contrasting images labelled Reason and Faith. The matter would be simple if we had to do with the clash between a mystic and a rationalist, between two worlds separated by a great gulf fixed. But was Erasmus a rationalist? It is true that he did all he could to encourage studies that developed the judgment, that he set great store by the efforts of man's reason, that he pricked the bubble of superstition and called on people to put their minds to the service of God. If it is to be a rationalist to trust in the use of common sense, to have an inkling of scientific law, to believe that God works by natural rather than supernatural means, to prefer the historical interpretation of scripture to the symbolic, to utilise reason in the investigation of truth on the assumption that revelation cannot run counter to reason though it may soar above it—then Erasmus may be called a rationalist. But if, as seems preferable, the term rationalist is to be kept within stricter limits —to denote one who trusts in reason above all things, who thinks that reason has the power and the duty to probe all depths and decide all questions, and who refuses to accept any other form of approach to truth —then Erasmus was decidedly no rationalist, as he was no sceptic. While he admired the results of the power of reason in the ancient writers, he deprecated them in the speculative philosophy of the Middle Ages, and this was because he thought that reason should not be the ultimate authority in matters of religion. True, some of the later medieval philosophers, notably Occam, had emphasised the antithesis between faith and reason and declared that reason was no guide in religious questions. But the essence of medieval philosophy was disputation; Erasmus and Luther were both trained in this school, and curiously enough it was Luther who threw the claims of reason fiercely aside, but who yet continued to debate on scholastic lines and to argue about matters of faith, while it was

Erasmus, the apostle of reasonableness if not of reason, who acted on his principles by urging that certain subjects should be treated as beyond the scope of logic.

It would be impossible here, even if it were within the competence of the writer, to attempt to go into all that lies behind the Erasmus–Luther controversy, and especially in the regions of theological debate. All we can hope to do is to attempt to arrive at an understanding of the forces of character involved, and an estimate of Erasmus's position in the struggle; and in doing so we shall necessarily have to sketch the process of deviation by which Humanism and the Reformation, at first so closely linked, came to array themselves against each other.

The similarities between Erasmus and Luther were at first so close as to blind anyone, even themselves, to their fundamental differences. Luther, some fifteen years younger than Erasmus, was also an Augustinian monk, though his entry into the monastery had been caused by some violent revulsion of spirit, after a brilliant beginning in the study of law. He was a perfect monk, labouring to fulfil all the duties of an arduous life, and like Erasmus, his support and consolation came from books, though in his case it was particularly the study of the Bible. He had not Erasmus's burning enthusiasm for antiquity, and his Greek never seems to have been carried very far. But he was quick to profit by the critical work of his contemporaries on the text of the Bible, such as that of Lefèvre d'Etaples and Erasmus himself; as soon as the text of the New Testament came out in 1516, Luther seized on it and made it the basis of his course of lectures on the Epistle to the Romans at Wittenberg, treating it however with some independence of mind. He was entirely at one with his humanist contemporaries in seeing the key to future development in the right understanding of the texts themselves, and for this purpose the study of the classical languages was essential, though to Luther it was always strictly a means to an end, without the fascination its artistic side had for Erasmus. It was in his own tongue that Luther was to be supremely eloquent, and his identification of himself with the German people provides an easy contrast to Erasmus's Latin cosmopolitanism. But in his beginnings, and to the outward eye, Luther was serving the same cause as the humanists.

His revulsion against medieval philosophy was as strong as Erasmus's. Both of them had been forced to delve into the heritage of the Schoolmen, in order to qualify for their University degrees, and in both the experience produced a lasting horror of the medieval outlook. But Luther was much more theologically minded than Erasmus, and his reaction was a more fundamental one. To Erasmus, sitting through the lectures in Paris and making fun of "Gryllard lecturing from his lofty chair," the stuff he was being asked to follow was merely contemptible; the later medieval philosophers such as Duns Scotus seemed to him equally laughable in form and content, their subjects of argument were so vapid, their methods so hair-splitting, and above all, their Latin so bad! That was the cardinal point: they disgraced the language of Virgil and Cicero. Erasmus certainly learnt enough medieval philosophy to "satisfy the examiners," but his mind was very little touched by it; his real studies were going on all the time behind the screen of scholastic theology, and as he read the great writers of antiquity he was preparing his own services to a Theology of a different order. In Luther's case this duality was hardly present. Luther read the Schoolmen hoping to discover truth; he must have plunged deeper into the study of the scholastics than Erasmus, for he began by taking them seriously as his masters, and his revulsion from them when he discovered his own point of view was correspondingly acute. He had lectured on them, much to his distaste, and as we have noticed already, their methods had sunk into his mind and he was inclined to use them, even in upholding a point of view diametrically opposed to theirs.

Luther had proclaimed his disagreement with scholastic theology before he stepped into the limelight with his condemnation of indulgences. The theses against the Schoolmen, and against the supremacy of Aristotle, proposed by Luther through his pupils as a subject of disputation in 1516 and 1517, were really more deeply significant of his personal point of view, than those ninety-five Theses against Indulgences which he posted up on the door of the castle church of Wittenberg on October 31st, 1517. But the practical issue was the one which caught public attention, as indeed Luther intended that it should. Here again, he seemed to be echoing Erasmus. He was not the first person to be shocked by the light-hearted profiteering from religious practices which was being indulged in at that time by the Church of Rome, or to condemn what one might call the mechanistic attitude to religion. Had not Erasmus, in his *Enchiridion Militis Christiani*, right at the beginning of the century, written

155

a sincere entreaty to all Christians not to put their faith in mechanical recitation of prayers and masses, kissing of relics, going on pilgrimage, but to try to substitute true charity for the Pharisaism of the time? And when Luther paid his visit to Rome, probably in 1510, Erasmus had only recently left the Eternal City, as much shocked by some aspects of it as Luther could well be. Differences there certainly were in the impact of Rome on those two powerful individualists. Erasmus, already well known, was received with open arms, and more important, with open libraries, by the learned Cardinals, and his memory of Rome was a mixed one, combining that luxurious welcome, that "fair and fragrant air," and the too-evident abuses and corruption of the Papal Court. He never forgot the sight of Julius II entering Bologna as a conqueror, and it was the un-Apostolic behaviour of the Popes rather than their extortions which horrified him. His weapon was satire, and the result of the Italian journey was *The Praise of Folly*. Compare with this picture the memory Luther had of himself, entering Rome as an obscure monk sent by his Order, with a naïve desire to turn this experience to the profit of his soul, and dropping on his knees at sight of the Holy City. He intended to make a complete confession of all the sins of his whole life, and to earn all the benefits promised to those who accomplished pious actions. So he found himself climbing up the steps to the Lateran, saying a paternoster at each step to earn for his grandfather's soul the indulgence promised at the top, and suddenly "coming to" with a great shock as he realised that he had doubts about the spiritual value of such a performance. Already at

156

that time he was beginning to have a glimpse of the revelation which was to underlie all his subsequent work, but his views needed several years of maturing before they were to be proclaimed to the world in the years following 1517.

The practice of indulgences was no new thing. It had gradually developed as part of the penitential system of the Church. Side by side with confession and contrition, penance had been recognised from early days, and in the Middle Ages it became the practice to make satisfaction for sins in some tangible form. The Crusaders were promised remission of sins or at least relaxation of penance; indulgences from penance were offered to people who contributed to the building of a church or founded a charity. The system was extended during the fourteenth century and in the fifteenth it included military and financial support in the war against the Turks and in rebuilding St. Peter's. "By the beginning of the sixteenth century the indulgence system had become one of the most productive devices of papal finance."[1] It was in the fifteenth century that the efficacy of this method of obtaining money was increased by the extending of the benefit of indulgences to souls in purgatory. Such a system could not fail to have its critics, and Luther was not alone in his condemnation of it. The Indulgence of 1515–17, which provoked his open attack, was one of the most scandalous of these devices to obtain cash for the Papal treasury. It was an Indulgence proclaimed throughout the lands of the Archbishop of Mainz, and the proceeds were, by a secret arrangement,

[1] Mackinnon, *Luther and the Reformation*, Longmans, London, 1925.

to be halved between the Archbishop and the Pope, for the express purpose of helping the Archbishop to pay for a dispensation which he needed to allow him to hold three high offices in the Church at once, while under the canonical age. This shady piece of work was camouflaged as a Jubilee indulgence for the building of St. Peter's, and contributors were promised a wide range of benefits, remission of all their sins however heinous, and remission for the dead as well as the living. No methods seem to have been too blatant for the indulgence preachers, especially the Dominican John Tetzel, who was the most successful of them all. It seems clear that these preachers did actually affirm that a mere money payment, apart from prayer or contrition, was enough to free a soul from purgatory, that they painted in lurid colours the agonies of their hearers' deceased relatives from which a small donation would set them free; and that a brisk trade in pardons was going on when Luther posted up his protest on the door of the Church at Wittenberg.

The consequences of this act have made it appear more dramatic than it was, an appeal to popular opinion or a manifesto. It was actually a perfectly normal proceeding, the announcement in the usual manner of a forthcoming academic disputation on the subject of punishment and repentance. Luther was led to it by his reading of the New Testament, and it was evidently by the help of Erasmus that he had come to realise that the words *poenitantiam agere* might have a different meaning than that given them by the Church. Instead of commanding the Christian to make satisfaction for his sins by the fulfilment of

158

certain works of penance, the precept meant "Repent ye"—rend your hearts and not your garments, undergo an inner change brought about by the grace of God. So far, in attacking the materialistic nature of the system of penance, Luther could be sure of the approbation of a spectator like Erasmus; he was speaking exactly in the vein of the *Enchiridion*. There were certainly differences of approach; Luther's was the direct and violent attack, Erasmus's the subtler rapier-thrust of ridicule. But there is no doubt that they would unhesitatingly have condemned the same vices and struggled equally to eliminate them.

*　　*　　*

Apparently, then, in 1517, Erasmus and Luther represented the same spirit of reform. Fundamentally the contrast was immense. It is well to see this clearly before beginning to study the actual tenor of their relations with each other, since the superficial likeness and the deep antagonism hold between them the key to the understanding of events. No two people could have approached these problems from more different angles or with more dissimilar experience.

The cardinal fact in Luther's life had been the hour of illumination in the tower-room of the monastery at Wittenberg, in 1512 or 1513, when there flashed upon him a new meaning of the words in Romans i, 16–17: "The just shall live by faith." Luther, one of the "twice-born," needed to reverse the direction of his whole life and be reborn into another vision of reality before he could begin his life-work. His years in the monastery had been a time of torment, not of intellectual frustration as in Erasmus's case, but of spiritual agony, because the beliefs which he had accepted from medieval theology were useless to satisfy his soul. The later Schoolmen, Duns Scotus and Occam, and their followers, who were Luther's first masters in theology, held that man, having free will in himself, can of his own accord, through baptismal grace, turn to God and thus merit the grace which leads to salvation. It is true, they said, that the salvation of man depends on the grace of God and His sovereign will, and the "merit" which man can acquire is only merit in so far as God is pleased to accept it as such. But he has endowed man with free will and has ruled that by exerting it in the right direction, by doing what in him lies to achieve the good life, man can earn or at any rate contribute to his own salvation. This doctrine depended on an optimistic view of human nature and minimised the power of evil and the effects of sin; it virtually did away with the conception of original sin as a fundamental corruption of man's nature, and it put a certain emphasis on the acts of the individual towards his own salvation, rather than on the saving of the world by the Redeemer. It is natural that such a doctrine should provide a foundation for a mechanistic view of religion, and as philosophy, however recondite, ends in influencing the masses, so there is a direct relation between the intricate theories of the schools and the exaggerated practices which both Erasmus and Luther condemned.

To Erasmus, however, the matter was a question of behaviour rather than of doctrine. Dogma was anathema to him. He was no theologian and knew it, and it was in the name of common sense alone that he had made his impassioned plea in the *Enchiridion* for the return to spiritual ideals. Anyone could see by the mere light of reason applied to the teaching of the Gospel, that God did not require ceremonies and observances, but purity of life, peace, brotherly love, an attempt, however feeble, to imitate the character of Jesus. Erasmus does not attempt to go into the doctrinal background of this simplified Christianity. His counsel presupposes certain things: a belief in man's latent power to do right when once enlightened, a close interaction between intelligence and ethical behaviour that is almost Cartesian. His introduction of the ancients into the education of a Christian is founded on the idea that their virtues, though unenlightened by Christian revelation, are still valuable and in their way God-given. If tackled on the question, Erasmus would have evaded the issue until it was no longer possible, when he would have retorted that, of course, all virtue and merit must ultimately derive from God. But he usually succeeded in evading all fundamental abstract problems, being eminently practical, especially interested in ethics and really very humble in face of the great mysteries of the spiritual world. He was one of the "once-born"; he began in the way he was to pursue for the rest of his life, and combined elements from different backgrounds to form what was for him a satisfactory working rule for living.

Clearly, if Erasmus hated the Schoolmen, it was not for their fundamental doctrines so much as for their methods and their "barbarism." With Luther it was otherwise. Luther, the inward-looking, was strongly conscious of the gulf which separated him from the righteousness of God; he lived his years in the monastery with the torments of a troubled conscience. His efforts to lead the good life, by fulfilling perfectly all that was required of him, put the philosophy he was taught to the test, and he found it wanting. He was acutely conscious that he *had not* in himself the power to do right, whatever the Schoolmen might say. No efforts of his own could wash away the consciousness of guilt from his soul. In his entourage, no one seemed to understand his restlessness: even the Vicar-General of his Order, John Staupitz, his kindly confessor, was unable to assuage his misery. He came to hate and fear the thought of a righteous God; he went through agonies of rebellion at the thought of the retribution which such a God was bound to visit on the guilty. Christianity as Luther came to conceive it in his period of trial was not a religion of love; it was full of terror and the sky was dark. The effort to discover the road to salvation, to a sense of oneness with the Divine, taxed all his powers and he felt it was completely unavailing.

So he struggled up to the day and hour when, after a long period of intense meditation on the passage of St. Paul in Romans i, 16–17, he had a sudden illumination. Hitherto the idea suggested to him by the phrase "the righteousness of God" had been that of retribution, of a just and terrible God who could not be placated by the puny satisfaction that man could make for his sins. His moment of illumination, as he himself explains it, revealed to him that "the righteousness of God revealed in the Gospel" could only be understood in connection with the following clause, "the just shall live by faith." That righteousness of the Gospel was not the righteousness of the law, the inexorable perfection before which no human soul can stand and which must needs punish the guilty; it was the gift of God to man, the righteousness which God mercifully imputes to the sinner, the garment with which He clothes the naked, the wealth He bestows on the indigent out of His own boundless treasure. Such righteousness has nothing to do with man's puny efforts towards virtue: they fade into non-existence in comparison with the great force of God's goodness. The illimitable power of redeeming Providence is substituted for the vain struggles of the soul. From a life of frustration and dissatisfaction with his own useless striving, Luther felt himself to be born again into a life of power; he was like a sinking swimmer, who feels his limbs giving way and his strokes growing weaker, when he is suddenly lifted up and swept to shore by the irresistible swell of the sea.

The idea which lifted Luther out of his personal misery and struck the weight from his shoulders, the doctrine of justification by faith and not by works, was, therefore, at the root of all his subsequent actions. In the light of it he re-read Scripture with a sense of freedom and joy. Not all at once, but gradually, he saw how profoundly it struck at the root of the medieval philosophy which had so failed to satisfy him. He now turned against the methods of Aristotle and the ideas of the Schoolmen with a passionate conviction, and in working out his own theology he was as dogmatic and as argumentative as his masters. It was a matter not of philosophy but of experience to him, that man is powerless to help himself until he is illumined by faith; he may wish to do right but he cannot, his will is enslaved, his understanding is dark, his inner conflict holds him bound, his virtue is derisory. It is strange that such a view of human nature should be the result and accompaniment of a psychological release, but so it is; to those like Luther the idea that all good is of God and comes through faith, and all human values are worthless in themselves, is a springing source of power and joy.

The process by which this regeneration is brought about by divine grace, transferring to the sinner the effects of the redemption of Christ, was the subject of Luther's commentaries as a lecturer on divinity, and he had already worked out his position by the time he sprang into prominence in 1517. He had discovered by then his mission as a Reformer. It is not possible for us here to go into the details of Luther's theological writings, but two points must be kept in mind for our purpose. One is that Luther's outlook necessarily included the negation of free will, and, therefore, was in direct antagonism not only to the later medieval philosophers but to the humanists. It was a curious fate that led Luther and Erasmus at the same time to attack the Schoolmen and such practices of their own age as the traffic in indulgences, and made them seem to be brothers-in-arms facing the same enemies, when in reality they were doing so from very different motives. When Erasmus condemned mechanical religious practices, he did so because he saw how they were substituted for ethical standards; he wished to see man's desire for salvation translated into a purer form of effort towards the good life. In other words, he thought the effort was valuable, if it was directed into intelligent instead of stupid channels, and that if the simple mind which treasured tangible relics could be led to treasure the precepts of Christ instead, a great advance would be made. But when Luther condemned indulgences, he did so from a deep conviction which counted not only these purely mechanical practices but all works as worthless; trust in indulgences was merely the most glaring instance of a faulty point of view. The higher and purer forms of moral effort, apart from a self-rejecting faith in the mercy of God, would fall for Luther under the same condemnation. And so, necessarily, all the works of antiquity would share the same fate.

The other point arising from Luther's premises which must not be forgotten, is that his view of the corruption of man's nature and man's own helplessness to correct it, led him to develop his belief in predestination. A logical outcome of the negation of free will, the doctrine of predestination is the furthest point of separation between humanist and reformer. It was taken up and developed later by Calvin, and the crystal-clear exposition of the whole doctrine in his *Institution de la Religion Chrétienne* (Latin, 1536, French 1541) marks the completion of the process by which the Revival of Learning and the Reformation branched away from each other. But it was really implicit in Luther's view of Christianity from the beginning. If man's will is vitiated and he cannot raise a finger to help himself, then it is without his volition that the gift of faith descends upon him, transforming his universe of sin into a place of redemption; he will certainly strive towards the good, but only as a result of this free gift of grace, which he cannot in any way attract or deserve. But sin is powerful in the world,

165

and only a certain number of people raise their heads towards the light; it was clear to Luther, following Augustine, that God in His inscrutable wisdom did not bestow the gift of grace on all, but only on the elect. Who they are, he said, and why they are chosen, it is not for man to know; and that any at all should be excepted from the just condemnation for sin, is an extraordinary effect of God's mercy. So the over-powering conviction of sin in Luther's mind led him to this inexorable doctrine, and separated him forever from humanist and Catholic; the one glorying in the inborn love of beauty and virtue in all mankind, the other believing that every baptised Christian has a gift of grace, enough to enable him to turn of his own free will to seek the aid of the Redeemer.

* * *

Thanks to Erasmus's letters, we can follow step by step, for nearly seven years, the history of his attitude to Luther, which began with discreet approval and ended with the decision to write against him the treatise on Free Will. This sounds as if a great change had occurred in Erasmus's mood and opinions, but actually the change was as minimal as it could well be; Erasmus's views were formed and his opinions changed very little. What changed was the state of the world round him. The radical nature of Luther's innovations in doctrine became clearer, the disapprobation of the See of Rome became more marked, the possibility of a split in the Church loomed up more terrifyingly—in fact, although attempts at reconciliation were repeatedly made during the first half of the century, the course of the Reformation with its

deep rift cutting across Christendom had become clear
by the time Erasmus died, even during those seven
years when he watched in such anxiety. During this
time Luther pounded on his way, apparently without
hesitation, discussing with the Papal Legate Cajetan
at the Diet of Augsburg in 1518, with Eck at Leipzig in
1519; condemned as a heretic by the Bull *Exsurge
Domine* in 1520, appearing before the Emperor at the
Diet of Worms in 1521 and boldly refusing to recant,
spirited away to the castle of the Wartburg to protect
his safety, returning in power to Wittenberg in 1522.
His convictions deepened, his antagonism and that
of his followers to their opponents grew more violent,
and the rift appeared more irremediable. Erasmus's
hopes of peace faded.

At the outset Erasmus had seen in Luther an estim-
able enthusiast engaged in the same struggle as
himself, but of doubtful discretion. As early as December 1516, Luther had prompted his friend Spalatin
to write to Erasmus, suggesting that the phrase in
Romans "the righteousness of the law" might mean
not simply ceremonies and pious practices, as Erasmus
took it, but the very keeping of the ten command-
ments—in fact, all human virtue, useless without
faith. Erasmus did not answer this inquiry from "an
Augustinian"—he was too busy defending himself
against Lefèvre d'Etaples, who had commented un-
favourably on a rendering in his New Testament.
It is curious how much of Erasmus's time during
those first years, when the storm of his life was blowing
up, was spent on learned quarrels which are of little
or no importance in the history of Europe.

He felt cordially disposed to Luther, however, and

some of Luther's friends were also his, especially Beatus Rhenanus and Philip Melancthon. In March 1519, there came a first letter from Luther, warm and deferential; (though it seems from other sources that Luther had already sensed the difference between his ideals and Erasmus's and judged that "human things have more weight with him than divine"). The letter was couched as from a disciple who wished to find an ally and a friend. Erasmus did not answer at once, but he wrote to the Elector of Saxony, in this time of Luther's peril, and asked him to protect the innocent; he was careful at the same time to dissociate himself from Luther's ideas. Writing to the gentle Philip Melancthon in April, he says all approve of Luther's character, but people vary about his opinions. "Why are there all these quarrels among learned men just now?" says Erasmus. "I consulted some astrologers, who say it is due to last year's eclipse, but I think it is the result of a conspiracy." A conspiracy against the New Learning, of course, and in most of his letters of 1519 and 1520 there is the same idea at the back of his mind. Good Letters are in danger.

At the end of May he replied to Luther's advances. It was a cool and prudent letter, though friendly, and must have caused keen disappointment to its more impulsive recipient. Erasmus said words failed him to describe the sensation aroused by Luther at Louvain, (where Erasmus had taken up residence and where he lived till 1521, with frequent journeys to other towns of the Netherlands in his capacity as Imperial Councillor, following the court of Charles V. It was not the best residence perhaps for his nerves, as the monks and theologians of Louvain were particularly loud in their aggressive protest against him and all he represented). He tells Luther how nothing can root out the unjustified conviction that Luther's works had an Erasmian inspiration, and that Erasmus was the standard bearer of the Lutheran party. "They thought they had been given a handle against good letters—which they hate, as attacking the majesty of theology, much more important in their eyes than Christ—and also against me, whom they regard as having contributed something to the cause of learning." How they rage and vociferate, he can hardly bring himself to describe. Erasmus knows that Luther's character is well spoken of, that in England and in Brabant there are those who approve of his writings, and they among the greatest. He himself neither approves nor disapproves: "I am keeping apart, as far as I can, so that I may the better serve the reflowering of Good Letters." He thinks more can be done by gentleness than by force, just as Christ conquered the world and as St. Paul turned disciples from the Jewish law. It would be better to complain of those who misuse the Pope's authority than of the Pope himself; the same in the case of kings; the schools are to be reformed rather than condemned. The essential thing is to keep free of anger or hatred or the desire for glory, things which creep insidiously into one's desire to serve religion.

He ended his letter on a warmer note, adding with the kindness of an older man to a younger, "I am not suggesting that you need this advice, but that you should go on doing what you do"—(words which were fastened on by his enemies, and needed the laborious explanation that for admonitions to be palatable they must be polite!) Erasmus praised Luther's commentary on the Psalms, mentioned some mutual friends, and ended with an Apostolic formula very unusual in his correspondence, and which shows how deeply he felt that much depended on Luther's acquiring a spirit of gentleness: "May the Lord Jesus daily impart His spirit more richly to you, to His own glory and the profit of mankind."

The first reading of this reserved letter gives the impression of a cold personality, keeping on the safe side and caring for nothing but knowledge. It is curiously less forthcoming than Erasmus's contemporary remarks to other correspondents about Luther. Probably it was a cold douche to the recipient. Yet on re-reading it one is struck by its dignity and calm and the prevalence of one note, the earnest hope of peace. It is not unfriendly, but far-sighted, and puts in the forefront the values which meant most to Erasmus, courtesy, self-control, the leisure to think, the practical virtues which are necessary to the service of God according to his lights. It may well stand representatively at the outset of his long and difficult relationship with the fiery Reformer.

The same day he wrote to John Lang, prior of the Augustinians at Erfurt: "Luther's freedom of action is loved by the best in the land (*optimi quique*); I have no doubt that his prudence will take care lest the affair should turn towards faction or rupture." It was more important, he added, to instil the mind of Christ into the minds of men than to fight with our fellow-Christians, and no victory could be expected unless the supremacy of the see of Rome and its satellites the Dominicans, Carmelites and Minorites was removed, and that could not be attempted without serious trouble. This was as far as Erasmus ever allowed himself to go after the advent of Luther.

During the rest of the year 1519 and throughout 1520 Erasmus's letters express the same point of view. He was surrounded by controversies and quarrels, defending himself against Lee in England and the enemies of the New Learning at Louvain, who persisted in regarding him as the instigator of all the contemporary attacks on the old theology. They ascribed to him not only Luther's activities but those of John Reuchlin, the German scholar who had made himself the champion of Hebrew against the monstrous proposals made at Cologne by a converted Jew named Pfefferkorn, that all Hebrew books except the Bible should be destroyed as contrary to Christianity. The proposal was a good example of the type of obscurantism that Erasmus had to contend with, and he was an interested spectator of the controversy it raised. In his letters of 1519 and 1520 Luther and Reuchlin are mentioned together because they were so often bracketed by their enemies, but Erasmus takes care to dissociate them from each other and himself from them, while protesting vigorously against the attempts to suppress and silence them that are daily being made.

In October 1519, he wrote to Albert of Brandenburg, in whose territories Luther was living, stating plainly the right of Luther to be heard, and if innocent, to be protected from oppression; if in error, to be gently admonished and corrected. "I would wish that heart, which seems to hold bright sparks of Gospel doctrine, not to be oppressed, but corrected and called to preach the glory of Christ. . . . The world is over-burdened with conventions of man's making, overburdened with the opinions and dogmas of the schools, overburdened with the tyranny of the mendicant orders. . . . I don't blame all of them, but many are of the sort who for the sake of power and gain bind in chains the consciences of men . . . They are now brazenly beginning to preach only their own notions and still more impudent doctrines, without a word of Christ." This, then, was what moved Luther. What else could it be, since he obviously did not aim at profit or personal glory? Erasmus shows how whenever Luther disputed a doctrine, the other party went as erroneously to the other extreme. He does not wish to be considered as belonging to the party of either Luther or Reuchlin, but he does see the difference between the old patient hearing of a heretic and the present mad raging against all unproven ideas.

Erasmus closes his letter by saying that he prefers to leave these cases to the decision of the tribunals that are sitting on them—Reuchlin's case having gone to Rome, Luther's to the Universities of Bâle, Louvain, Freiburg and Paris. Let them decide: it is not Erasmus's responsibility. "I have always taken care not to write anything obscene, or seditious, or foreign to the doctrine of Christ. Never will I willingly become a teacher of error or a leader of revolt. I am ready to hear anything rather than awake rebellion."

That was one thing at least of which he was perfectly sure: he would not lend himself to the division of Christendom. In his preface to the *Colloquiorum Formulae* of 1519 he wrote: "I am a Christian and I acknowledge Christians; I will make no Erasmists and I know no Reuchlinists," and equally no Lutherans. (He was thinking, no doubt, of the rebuke of St. Paul in 1 Corinthians i, 12: "every one of you saith, I am of Paul; and I of Apollos; and I of Cephas; and I of Christ. Is Christ divided? Was Paul crucified for you? or were ye baptised in the name of Paul?") There is plenty of evidence in these letters of 1519 and 1520 that Erasmus felt great sympathy for Luther; he admitted, and not only to Luther's friends, that the preacher of Wittenberg had great powers, and was sincere in his efforts to serve religion, a man to be listened to and dealt with fairly. No one could have been more alive than Erasmus to the need of reform. He saw the whole thing, too, as an extension of the war against the New Learning, inspired by the hatred of the narrow-minded for those classical studies which were ousting them from their scholastic supremacy. The same loud and virulent enemies were attacking him, Lefèvre d'Etaples and Luther indiscriminately; in 1521 he is repeating with a bitter smile the story of the Carmelite who preached in the presence of the King of France and said that Anti-Christ was coming and had sent on ahead four precursors, "some Minorite in Italy, Lefèvre in France, Reuchlin in Germany, Erasmus in Brabant"— Luther presumably being the central figure. There was plenty of reason to think that in most people's minds they were identified, especially as the public burning of Luther's books in the autumn of 1520, was accompanied by violent attacks on Erasmus, particularly at Louvain; the deed being done by the Papal Legate, Erasmus's former friend Aleander. The idea of leaving Luther unprotected to the attacks of such people horrified Erasmus and he did his best to prevent it, as far as his influence would go, both by letters and direct proposals, though at the same time he advised Froben against printing Luther's books.

It was during this same autumn of 1520 that his activity in favour of Luther was the greatest; he was back at Louvain after assisting at the brilliant scenes following the election of Charles V as Emperor, and paying his court to Henry VIII at Calais, where the English King had come for the interview with the Emperor at the Field of the Cloth of Gold. Erasmus also saw More on this occasion, and shook hands with his English adversary Lee, who was there too. Erasmus was not well—he says in one letter: "last summer's hot weather nearly finished me"—but he was as busy as ever, and amid all his labours keeping an eye fixed on the fate of Luther. The Bull *Exsurge Domine* perturbed him deeply. It seemed like a victory for the obscurantists. "I am deeply disturbed about the wretched Luther," he wrote. "If they pull this off, no one will be able to bear their insolence. They will not be quiet until they have utterly ruined the study of languages and Good Letters . . . This tragedy has sprung from the hatred of Good Letters and the stupidity of the monks."

On September 13th, 1520, he wrote to the Pope. It was a difficult letter to write. Luther had already been proclaimed a heretic, and tentative suggestions had come through to Erasmus from the direction of the Vatican, indicating that if he were to take up his mighty pen and crush Luther, there would be a bishopric for him if he wished . . . He had no intention at this point of doing any such thing, but he had no intention either of joining forces against the Pope. It called for all his powers of tact and management to convey, as he did, a graceful refusal of these blandishments, and to admit that he had favoured Luther and still thought that he should be judged impartially. He repeats that the whole affair has arisen from the hatred of "languages and good letters, as they are called," and urges that if Luther's opponents had first refuted his arguments and then burnt his books, they might have had some effect. As it is, Erasmus plainly thinks that persecution only makes matters worse, and a phrase recurs here which often comes under his pen: "Free and lofty minds are willing to be taught, but refuse to be coerced."

He could speak more plainly to the Rector of the University of Louvain, on whose protection he had to rely against the slanders of his theological opponents. To him he urged more strongly that Luther should not be condemned unheard; even the Bull gives him time to repent. "No one stands out who will soberly and learnedly reply to Luther, without the interference of ignorance, laziness or fear." Erasmus himself is not the man for the job: he gives several reasons for this, one being that his hands are full with his chosen work, and he cannot spare the time to go into these matters of dogma and read not only what Luther has written but what others have written too. Then he frankly does not want to incur the hatred of so many people as this would involve. More important perhaps, he does not wish to set himself up to judge another man's creed. This, one feels, was the bedrock truth. "I recognise my own mediocrity," he wrote, "or rather the slenderness of my capacity (*tenuitas*)." In other places he refers to the taunt that he is merely a grammarian and nothing else : it may be so, and in that case, why clamour against him for not engaging in theological controversy? Even his learned adversary the "Camel" (the Carmelite Egmondanus) cannot have it both ways.

No, "I would rather be a spectator than an actor in this play"—but that does not prevent him from making several definite attempts towards a positive contribution. On November 5th, 1520, he had an interview with the Elector Frederick of Saxony at Cologne. The Elector asked him if he considered Luther had erred. "Yes," said Erasmus, "in two points : he has attacked the Pope's crown and the monks' bellies." An epigram would not satisfy the questioner, so Erasmus grew more serious and drew up twenty-two Axioms stating that the best solution would be for the Pope to recommend the decision of the matter to a tribunal of learned and impartial men. About the same time he wrote a number of letters introducing a Dominican, John Faber of Augsburg, who finally took with him to the Diet of Worms in 1521, a proposal of arbitration, "Counsel of one heartily desiring the peace of the Church," which was clearly the result of collaboration with Erasmus.

To More, in that same November 1520, he wrote a long and amusing description of his disputation with Egmondanus, the "Camel," in the presence of the Rector of Louvain. He was told then that it was he, Erasmus, who put Luther into men's minds, that it was he who taught Luther how to write : "You wrote for Luther, now write against him." "The theologians think," he wrote to another friend, "that Luther

176

cannot be stopped except by my pen, and they privately beg me to write against him. But far be it from me to be as mad as that."

On the contrary, one of the last letters of 1520, is another attempt to influence the Vatican in Luther's favour, a long letter to the Cardinal Campeggio whom Erasmus had known at Rome. It is perhaps the clearest expression of his own views.

Erasmus persists in thinking that the matter is essentially a dispute between the supporters of the Old Learning and those of the New: both are at fault in their attitude and methods. "This then is the source and seedbed of the whole of this tragedy, the ineradicable hatred of languages and good letters. The scene may vary, the actors and the characters may change, but it is the same play all the time." Then he turns to the question of Luther.

"Of all Luther's books I have read less than a dozen pages, and those here and there; and yet out of these, skimmed through rather than read, I seemed to detect in the author rare gifts of nature, a mind finely endowed for expounding the mysteries of Scripture after the style of the old writers, and for kindling the spark of Gospel doctrine; from which there has been a great falling away, both on account of public morals and of the methods of the schools, too intent on subtleties rather than on the essential questions. I heard excellent men, who had examined the doctrine and the faith of Luther, congratulating themselves that they had happened to meet with these books. I saw that it was the people of most upright life and nearest to the purity of the Gospel who were least offended by Luther.

Then his character was praised even by those who could not stomach his doctrine. And also, I preferred to take a favourable rather than an unfavourable view of the spirit of the man, of which God only can judge. Finally, the world seemed to be weary of the old doctrines too much concerned with little human ideas and constitutions, and to be thirsting for the pure living draught drawn from the sources of Evangelists and Apostles; and this man seemed to me suited for this work, both by natural gifts and ardour for study.

"Thus, then, did I favour Luther; I favoured the good that was in him or that I believed to be in him, yet it was not him I favoured, but Christ's glory. And yet I saw much in him that awoke my anxiety and suspicion. So when he approached me by letter of his own accord, I at once took the opportunity to admonish him and say what I wished him to avoid, so that his mind, corrected and purified, might most fruitfully and to the great glory and service of Christ, reinstate for us the philosophy of the Gospel, now almost moribund (*frigescentem*)."

Erasmus goes on to give the reasons for moderation that he gave to Luther, mainly in the name of expediency. "Let us judge on the facts," says Erasmus. "St. Paul spared the false apostles. How much more should we avoid violence against one whose purity of life is admired by all, whose books are the delight of so many excellent and noble men, so many of the pious and learned!" So far, he says, Luther could hardly have been treated worse.

*　　*　　*

However, during 1521, there are signs in his correspondence of growing exasperation with Luther. From the beginning Erasmus had mistrusted his fiery spirit, and that of some of his friends; a letter from the young nobleman Ulrich von Hutten in August 1520, had shown which way the wind was blowing. Hutten had been a great favourite and admirer of Erasmus, and through his adherence to Luther was to become one of his bitterest enemies. His letter showed how Erasmus's judicial attitude had annoyed Luther's friends, and how powerful they still judged him to be for good or ill. Then Luther had written a good deal during 1520, and the violence of his books, especially the one *On the Babylonian Captivity*, had sickened Erasmus. In November came another inflammatory letter from Hutten, summoning Erasmus to join himself and Luther, breathing fire and slaughter against Pope and Emperor, telling Erasmus that his life was not safe and mentioning poison, talking about dying for liberty and "let us remember we are Germans . . ." But that his letter is preserved, one can imagine Erasmus picking it up gingerly by the corner and transferring it to the wastepaper basket, for it was all he most disliked. As for the mention of Germans, over and over again at this time Erasmus speaks of the primitive fierceness and savagery characteristic of the Germans; they love war for its own sake. In his lighter mood he says: "If this goes on, I shall choose to be a Frenchman," alluding to the discussion as to whether the Low Countries (and his birthplace) are to be counted as part of Germany or France.

The position was becoming more than embarrassing.

On the one hand there were the well-known abuses of the Church and the indescribable vulgarity and fury of Luther's enemies; (the atmosphere of Louvain had become unbearable to Erasmus and he had now removed to Bâle). On the other, the increasing fury and arrogance of Luther himself and his friends. Erasmus wrote in despair, "Luther has covered us and good learning with hatred. Everyone knows that the Church is overburdened with abuse of authority and ceremonies and man-made decrees for the purpose of gain. Many people are now wishing for a remedy, but often an imprudent attempt at a cure makes things worse. I wish that man had either been more moderate or else left things alone!" "What a mass of hatred Luther is bringing down on good learning and Christendom! He is trying to involve everyone in his affairs." "As to your counsel to join Luther, I will if I see him on the side of the Catholic Church . . . and there Erasmus will be found, where there is the peace of the Gospel." Erasmus was, in fact, in a bad dilemma, hating both extreme parties and hated by both. "Those who appear to favour Luther, have tried in all possible ways to get me on their side. Those who are against him have tried to push me into his party, raging in public sermons against my name more violently than against Luther himself. I, however, am not to be moved from my attitude of mind by any machination. I acknowledge Christ, I do not know Luther."

For the first time Erasmus now mentions a matter of doctrine. "They say Luther got some of his ideas out of my books. What could be a more impudent lie? since the very first article (of Luther's *Assertio*)

THE LUTHERAN TRAGEDY

plainly refutes their futility. Where do I say that
everything we do is sin?" Later, in May 1521, he
explains how Luther has pushed to an extreme what
he himself advocated in moderation. He tried to deter
people from rash vows, vain pilgrimages, too early
entry into monastic orders; Luther condemns all
vows. Erasmus has said confession is sometimes burd-
ensome; Luther rejects it totally—and so on. He
has robbed Erasmus's work of much of its fruit. He has
put a weapon into the hands of those who rage against
good learning, and against good men who favour
the Gospel doctrine in simplicity of heart. A fine
champion of evangelical liberty! His writings have
clinched the matter, and made the evil irremediable.
He seems to act as though he courted destruction.
As for Erasmus, he is "stoned" all the time, not once
for all like St. Stephen, but over and over again with
the violent accusations of his enemies.

He knew, moreover, that he was not either temper-
amentally or physically suited to battling for a creed.
He was an old man now, frequently ill, and as he said
in a letter to Lord Mountjoy, his old Maecenas,
"No one knows better than you how I have always
loved peace." Frankly he admits that he does not
think he is of the stuff of the martyrs, and if a great
disturbance were to occur, he would be most likely to
take St. Peter's way.

The truth perhaps lay neither in differences of
doctrine nor in Erasmus's modest refusal of the
martyr's crown. The fact was that Erasmus believed in
education, Luther in revelation. The notion that
one article of faith suddenly perceived could alter
life and in itself save a man's soul, was outside and

contrary to Erasmus's experience. To him the Christian life was a growing in knowledge, a progressive enlightenment and above all a way to nobler living. For this one must have time, quiet of mind, freedom to concentrate one's powers; his ideal necessitated peace. He was not sure that dogma as we see it can embrace truth, and he was certain that one man's truth is not always another's. His position is clearly expressed in a letter of 1519:

"Such is human mentality, that we cling desperately to anything that has once been defined. However, the philosophy of Christ rests on this one thing, that we should understand that in God is all our hope, and that He bestows everything on us through His Son Jesus. By His death we are redeemed, by baptism we have become members of His body, so that dying to worldly desires we may live after His precept and example . . . and so we may go on from strength to strength, but not taking any merit ourselves but ascribing all good to God.

"The thing is to teach people those things until they become second nature. If anyone wants to work out more abstruse questions about the hypostasis of Christ in some of the sacraments, and so uplift the mind to sublime things, let him do so; but preserve us from the state of things in which everyone is bound to take up at once as an article of faith what has seemed true to this or that other person . . . Let us not be afraid to say: 'God knows how it is done, it is enough for me to believe.'"

The difference between Erasmus and the Schoolmen stands out clearly here, as does that between Erasmus and Luther.

As time went on, the violence of Luther and his party, and perhaps an increasing consciousness of the fundamental nature of the differences between them, hardened Erasmus to the reformer's cause. At the beginning of 1521, a letter from the Pope had conveyed plain though guarded suggestions that he should take up his pen against Luther. But that was still impossible to him, for it would have meant appearing to side with Luther's opponents, and they were the very people whose attacks against himself he was having to parry on all sides. Another adversary sprang up during 1521; the Spanish theologian Zúñiga, (Stunica), a professor at Alcala and one of the authors of the Polygot Bible called the Complutensian. He had brought out critical notes against Erasmus's translation of the New Testament as well as against Lefèvre, and unhesitatingly accused Erasmus of ignorance and heresy. Erasmus had in fact two classes of opponent, the learned die-hards who objected to his methods of exegesis and his denunciation of medieval theology, and the ignorant monks who feared his lashing exposure of their vices and their methods of imposing on the public. Both groups were equally vociferous in their vituperation. The only thing to do was to carry the war into their camps, and in 1522, this was what Erasmus proceeded to do, by editing all his defensive writings against Lee, Stunica and others in a volume of *Apologiae omnes* published by Froben, and on the other hand by publishing a new edition of the *Colloquies*. These burst on the world in March 1522, transformed from a handful of instructive Latin exercises into the first of the brilliant and amusing collections of dialogues that we know today. They contained some clear pictures of the Christian life as Erasmus saw it, simple in its ideals, indifferent to ceremonies and practices, treasuring the wisdom of the ancients together with the philosophy of Christ. In the second edition in August 1522, stood the *Religious Banquet*, re-written in its final form and breathing a wonderful serenity in the midst of these conflicts.

Two of Erasmus's circle of friends had caused a scandal in Bâle by breaking the Lenten fast. He took the opportunity to write a short essay on abstinence (*De Esu Carnium*) which he addressed to the Bishop of Bâle. In it he proposed various practical reforms, reduction of the number of saints' days, permission for priests to marry, toleration in the matter of feasts and abstinence. In his *Apology to Carranza*, another critic, and his second *Apology to Stunica*, he defined his moderate attitude, his desire for certain reforms, his reliance on the Gospel itself for the fundamental articles of belief. At the same time he was having to defend himself against the theologians of Louvain who professed to be scandalised by the freedom of the *Colloquies*; they produced passages casting doubt on the Scriptural authority for vows, indulgences, confession and fasting. On both sides Erasmus saw himself threatened with trial for heresy, a terrible fate which seemed at times very close to him. He could defend himself by his pen, as he continued to do with vigour, and the great ones of the earth—Charles V, the Cardinals, Henry VIII, Francis I—remained favourable to him. But the great question remained: would the Pope support him? He had sent to Adrian VI his text of *Arnobius on the Psalms*, with a dedicatory letter, and an appeal to the Pope not to judge him on the slanderous accusations of his enemies until his defence had been heard. In December, uneasy because the Pope's reply was delayed, he sent another copy, with a letter offering to suggest in secret a means of quieting the dispute. He did not regret anything that he had written, but apologised if the language used was sometimes too bold: the time is not now for amusement but for watchfulness. "I see the danger closer than I could wish, or than many people understand. May Christ bring it all to a good end!"

But the Pope had already written to him on December 1st. The Brief contained an acknowledgement of *Arnobius* in gracious terms, and also a command to take up his pen and write against the new heresies, "as for many reasons you ought to consider this domain especially reserved for you by God; for you have great power of mind, varied learning, swiftness in writing, such as in our memory, few others have had, not to say none." He would never find a better opportunity of serving Christendom, than by confuting the old heresies rejuvenated by Martin Luther. Let him not say that he is unequal to the task. And the letter closed with a warm invitation to come to Rome, once the winter was over and the city purged of the plague which was then infesting it; "come as soon as you can, but well and happy." The Pope himself and all Erasmus's Roman friends will welcome his arrival, and libraries will be open to him and there will be every opportunity of discussing these events with pious and learned men. In a later letter the Pope approved his suggestion of offering a solution to the troubles of Christendom, "for there is nothing under the sun which we more ardently desire." He renewed his invitation to go to Rome. There was no doubt now as to the course Erasmus was expected to take, from the point of view of the Vatican.

And yet, after Luther's disappearance from the scene, after his spectacular refusal to recant at the Diet of Worms, his followers had expected Erasmus to step into leadership in his place. Durer wrote in his diary: "O Erasmus of Rotterdam, where wilt thou abide? O thou knight of Christ, seize the martyr's crown!" "I am a heretic to both sides," commented Erasmus.

The cards were now on the table, and on March 22nd, 1523, Erasmus replied to the Pope. In the least offensive way that he could, Erasmus refused both the invitation to Rome and the request to write against Luther. A ferocious tyrant, he said, had issued an edict that he was not to travel: his name was *Calculus*, the stone. As to writing against Luther, he thought it useless; his credit was gone in Germany, and he had no wish to bring down on himself so much hatred to no purpose. He was in no way linked with the Lutherans, but he judged the present tumult too grave to be put down by coercive measures; true, the Wyclifites had been oppressed by fire and sword in England, but not suppressed, and it would be still more difficult to apply force to a movement in Germany, cut up as it was into so many small principalities. A better method would be the mild and clement one, suited to the Pope's own character; examination of the sources of the evil, proclamation of an amnesty, application of a provisional disciplinary truce in the

186

states and towns affected, supervision of the press. But also the world could be promised the hope of certain alleviations and reforms: the head of the Church could pronounce the magic word of Liberty. To examine the origins of the trouble, decide on the reforms and define the liberty of consciences, let there be convened a council of serious, incorruptible and unbiassed, merciful-minded men.

This letter represented the last phase of Erasmus's effort to heal the wounds of Christendom without entering into acrimonious dispute. But it was already too late.

Perhaps Erasmus knew that he was being too optimistic in recommending to the Pope a course of action which would have cancelled out two severe steps already taken, the Bull *Exsurge Domine* and the Edict of Worms. He knew at all events that he would have in the end to break his silence and pronounce something on the Lutheran question, but he did not intend it to be an attack on Luther; for some time he had been thinking about a little book, not against Luther, but on peace. In the *Catalogue of Writings* which he prepared for his friend John Botzheim of Constance, in the winter of 1522–3, there is a detailed description of this work, which was never finished. It was to have been a three-cornered discussion, a new Colloquy of a serious kind, or rather three Colloquies, between a supporter of Luther (Thrasymachus) an opponent (Eubulus) and an arbitrator (Philalethes). The first dialogue was to examine the question of whether the matter of reform ought to be tackled in the Lutheran way, even if all Luther's assertions were proved to be true. The second would discuss his doctrines, or some of them, and the third would show how this disturbance could be quieted, in such a way that it would not easily start up again. "The affair will be discussed by the two of them, without accusations and strife, without deceit; simple and naked truth will be put forward, with such fairness and moderation that I think the danger will be that the opposite party (the Catholic) will be angrier with me than Luther, interpreting my indulgence as collusion." This would have been a truly Erasmian approach: "I see that severity is more pleasing to some people," he said, "but in my method every person is allowed to be pleased with his own judgment. It is easier to be severe, but to my mind this is the better way."

Why did Erasmus abandon this piece of work, which would now be the most precious of commentaries on the Lutheran question? And why, in the course of a few weeks in the summer of 1523, did he finally yield to the appeals of his friends and begin a treatise directed against Luther? The first question is easy to answer; he found by simply announcing that he was writing a free discussion of the Lutheran problem, that it would have angered all sides and that no country in Europe was ready to turn to the Erasmian way of thinking. Even his English friends disapproved. The opposition of Paris or Louvain was unquestionable, and there was no sign of support from the Pope. (In any case Adrian VI was never to reply to Erasmus's letter: he died on September 14th.) Even the Lutherans were hostile to the project, considering it a veiled form of attack. Finally Erasmus gave it up and probably destroyed the scheme. He had still not agreed to write against Luther. What made him change his mind? There is no direct evidence about this; but it is clear that the storm was rising, that the powerful Sorbonne was adding its attacks to those of Stunica and the hostile theologians of Louvain, that it was becoming necessary to state where one stood under pain of being accused of heresy. And from England came a letter from Thomas More (now lost). What arguments did it contain? Some strong reasoning put forward by Erasmus's friends, some new illustration of the gulf widening between his views and Luther's, broke down his opposition, and he began to sketch out his *Essay on Free Will*.

* * *

One cannot help feeling that the *Essay on Free Will* was a *pis aller* for Erasmus. There were three possible ways of entering into the conflict. One was to continue his own method of witty, popular discussion: this would have been most suited to his character, but he had abandoned it with the scrapping of the three dialogues. Another way was to associate himself actively with the attempt of the new Pope Clement VII, to find means of pacifying the conflict; he was, in fact, invited by the Cardinal Legate Campeggio, his old friend, to meet him at Augsburg and give him counsel. But Erasmus shrank from active measures: the opportunity had come too late, and age and increasing physical distress emphasised his natural aversion to conflict and his distrust in himself. He chose the third way, least suited to his genius, least attractive and least efficient: the treatise on a

189

theological subject, addressed to his own wide admiring public but less likely to appeal to them than to a small audience of theologians, and dealing with an abstract question rather than with the warm and simple creed with which he had identified his name.

However, when the *Essay on Free Will* came out (September 1524) it must have been an uncommon surprise for most of its readers. It succeeded almost as well as the three dialogues could have done in enraging one and all of the extremists.

The Lutherans, in any case, were bound to take it as a hostile act. Erasmus had come slowly to the resolution to write it and was never very happy about the whole matter; while he announced his decision to Rome and England, he concealed it as long as possible from his German friends. As we have seen, he was determined not to be in Luther's camp but reluctant to be among his enemies. Luther wrote to him proposing (somewhat contemptuously) a pact of non-aggression—neither of them to write against the other; but that did not suit Erasmus's idea of personal freedom. This last correspondence of Erasmus and Luther has been acutely analysed by M. Renaudet, who notes how Luther, like Hutten, could not imagine any motive for the moderation and pacific spirit of Erasmus except base and selfish ones; how he writes to Erasmus in the tone of a prophet addressing a man incapable of spiritual insight: "I have tolerated your weakness and respected in you a measure of the gifts of God." The cause, he said, was beyond the scope of an Erasmus and had nothing to fear from his opposition. But if he would be silent and remain a spectator, Luther also would refrain from attacking him. . . . Erasmus replied with frankness: what Luther called his weakness was reflection. He had always experienced in reading Luther's works a double impression of truth and falsehood. For Luther to write against him was perhaps the best thing that could happen to him, for it would at last convince his enemies that they were not hand and glove. The fact that Luther proposed such a pact of silence, and that the correspondence was soon an open secret, made the writing of the *Essay on Free Will* a necessity. The Lutheran party was on tiptoe, waiting for the sign of open war, ready for the bite of the acid from the most caustic of pens, already raging against Erasmus as the traitor to their cause. Luther himself remarked that one bite from Erasmus was worse than being devoured by all the Papists at once.

On the other hand there were the ranks of the orthodox, from the Pope downwards: the Cardinals who expected him to speak vigorously in support of the authority of the Church, the King of England who had already entered the lists against Luther, the English friends and above all Thomas More, expecting a defence of orthodoxy; and there were the vulture-eyed flocks of Erasmus's chief enemies, the monks and the academic theologians, waiting to pounce upon new proofs of his heretical tendencies, only willing to disculpate him if he were to publish a defence of them and all their works, indulgences, enforced celibacy, compulsory confession, relic-worship and the like. Only by such a whole-hearted recantation could Erasmus have placated Paris and Louvain.

When they opened the *Essay on Free Will* these latter

gentry must have choked with rage. Not for nothing had Erasmus written to his friends: "Whatever happens, I shall remain myself." His answer to Luther held no resounding defence of Rome and all its works, no challenge on the grounds of Luther's innovations, no wholesale condemnation. It was a quiet examination of the Scriptural evidence for and against belief in Free Will, and he treated this excommunicated heretic as gently as if he had been his brother. This tone of conciliation was strictly in harmony with Erasmus's consistent attitude in face of the widening schism, but it infuriated equally both Luther and his enemies.

THE ESSAY ON FREE WILL

Erasmus began his essay with a statement of his often-repeated conviction that there are some truths which remain hidden to us, some questions on which we should be content to know only a little. Deep subjects of religious controversy may be debated in conference or in the schools, but they should not become matters of public discussion. However, since Luther has brandished his convictions in the face of the world, and Erasmus wishes to see truth victorious, he is willing to discuss the question of free will, but as a critic and not as a judge.

Luther professes to disregard all opinions but his own. This releases Erasmus from the necessity of going over all the writings of past authors on this subject, and he accepts with joy the restriction of the subject to the actual words of the Bible. He does, however, prefix to his analysis of Scripture a short history of the doctrine of Free Will, explaining to the inexperienced reader the differences between the

Augustinian view of Grace and the Pelagian, the one attributing all good in man to the action of Grace without any co-operation on the human side, the other exalting the idea of Free Will so far as to claim that man once delivered from original sin can of his own accord choose eternal life. After a short scholarly discussion of these two points of view, Erasmus plunges into the study of the Biblical evidence, first quoting passages in support of the possession by man of free will, then taking one by one the passages which Luther alleges to be proofs against it.

The method he follows is very markedly his own. Though he does not despise tradition as Luther does—having the greatest admiration for some of the Fathers of the Church—he relies entirely in his argument on reason and common sense. It is repellent to him to think of God as cruel, as exacting service and obedience from a creature deprived of all power to render these things, and he finds it absurd that the Scriptures should be full of admonitions to choose the true way of life, to strive, to repent, if none of this is possible to the enslaved will of man. Most of all his humanist's conscience revolts at the idea of predestination, which takes away all semblance of freedom from the human soul and turns it into an automaton or a puppet. The matter in hand lay at his heart and he treats it with great sincerity. Some of his illustrations have a quiet poetic beauty, for instance his use of the story of the Prodigal Son to illustrate the relation between the soul and God: "and he arose, and came to his father. But when he was yet a great way off, his father saw him, and had compassion, and ran, and fell on his neck, and kissed him. . . ." So the little effort of which man's free will is capable is met by the great power of the love of God.

One thing is very marked in Erasmus's dealings with the Bible: he always treats it as a textual critic, that is, he remains aware of the context, the historical circumstances, and the time and place of each text that he examines. It is important, he says, to consider the position and meaning of the parable, otherwise one is in danger of misapplying it. The thing that one must not do is to isolate a text and build on it, poised *in vacuo*, a whole structure of doctrine—precisely, in fact, what Luther does. Luther will take St. Paul's metaphor of the potter and the clay, and his reference to the great house where there are "vessels to honour and vessels to dishonour," and extract from that a proof of predestination; but when St. Paul goes on to say: "if a man purge himself from these, he shall be a vessel unto honour, sanctified, and meet for his Master's use," the metaphor breaks down and so does its value as evidence for lack of free will. For how could the earthen pot turn itself into gold or purify itself for the Master's use? Erasmus explicitly states his view that the best way to understand Scripture is to examine the central idea of the passage, and then relate what touches on it in the parables and metaphors to this central theme.

To the dispute as to whether God's grace or man's choice operates in the conversion of the sinner, Erasmus brings as usual an intermediate theory. Just as the general is said to win the battle, but the soldiers are not unimportant, or the architect is said to build the house, but the bricklayers have done their part, so in all good actions the inspiration and the completion are of God, but man co-operates by opening his mind to God's grace. Erasmus distinguishes three parts in each action: the initial inspiration, the continuation and the successful achievement, and says that the middle term is the only one in which man's free will is of any avail.

This is in all essentials the doctrine of Thomas Aquinas, that man cannot merit grace in the first place, nor achieve by himself final perfection, but he may earn by his striving the increase of grace already received. M. Pierre Mesnard, who recently edited the essay, sums up the position:[1] "The theology of Erasmus rests in fact on the central idea of divine perfection. An all-powerful God, of infinite goodness, has shown forth both his power and his goodness in the order of creation. His creatures owe him everything; it is thus an insult to their creator to cast a doubt on the consubsistent reality of the natural order. But out of His excessive goodness and in spite of the rejection of His first advances, God endows man with the possibility of obtaining the exceptional privilege of final blessedness: to reach it, the fallen nature of man is doubly in need of being infused with supernatural life. This is the work of Grace, which restores nature and carries it beyond itself by enlightening and strengthening free will. Thus man has received everything from God, but this does not prevent him from being Man, and while he considers himself an unprofitable servant, he yet shows in his behaviour the dignity of a free and reasoning agent, created in the image of God." This doctrine, which is the orthodox Catholic view, was probably

[1] P. Mesnard, *Essai sur le Libre Arbitre*, Paris, 1945, p. 60.

taken by Erasmus direct from Thomas Aquinas.

Erasmus wished to preserve the belief in free will and at the same time to avoid the over-confidence in works which produced the abuses of his day, "thus keeping the principal advantages of the Lutheran doctrine." He ended by saying that his conclusion did not in any way invalidate all that Luther had written in a devout and Christian vein on the great goodness of God, or the necessity of abandoning all presumption on our own merits, and placing all our confidence in God's promises. In conclusion, Erasmus was not unwilling to learn from a younger man; but if he had erred all his life in his understanding of the truth of Christianity, what about all the Fathers of the Church? Had they all been wrong too?

So ended the *Essay on Free Will*, less a treatise on theological doctrine than an attempt to find justification in Scripture for the sense of the dignity of man. It was only reluctantly that Erasmus ever approached theological questions. Here, in a piece of writing wrenched from him by the circumstances of his time, we find him like himself, still expressing the double trend of his mind; on the one hand the dislike of intellectual analysis applied to matters of spiritual import, on the other the humanistic belief in the dignity and high destiny of man. He was the same person as the boy who had devoured the classics so eagerly and yet imbibed without knowing it the teaching of the Brethren of the Common Life.

* * *

To present the world with the *Essay on Free Will* in 1524, was like asking two duellists seething with hatred to put up their swords and admire the view. It was received favourably by the Pope and by Erasmus's English friends, and some of Luther's more moderate allies like Philip Melancthon were attracted by it and grateful for its moderation. But it could not please the extremists on either side. The militant Catholic party found it too gentle, and in any case it did not tackle Luther on the right things. Erasmus remained suspect, the more so because every step he took in his controversy with Luther was accompanied by a new issue of the *Colloquies*, each one more exasperating to the monks than the last. It was as if he were quite determined to show that agreeing to write against one of Luther's doctrines did not mean that he was not fully in agreement with Luther about the practical reforms needed in the Church. "Erasmus could easily see that the Catholics would have been better pleased with him if, instead of offering courteously to hold an academic debate with Luther on a point of religious psychology, he had openly attacked the Lutheran doctrine on indulgences, sacraments, the pre-eminence of Rome. But this was just what he had not wished to do."[1] In fact, he was not interested in defending the views of Luther's enemies, but only his own.

Luther himself met the graceful little book with a bomb. His reply, the *De Servo Arbitrio*, appeared at Wittenberg in December 1525. In this large tome, which embodied some of Luther's strongest opinions, the Reformer let his pen go and used even stronger language than usual. He calls Erasmus names in the grand manner: he is a babbler, a sceptic, a Lucian

[1] Renaudet, op. cit., p. 237.

197

"or some other hog from the Epicurean sty," his book is stupid, impious, blasphemous, ignorant and hypocritical, and the doctrine it preaches is prettily compared to glue, mud and garbage. Luther scouts the idea that any theological problem should be unsuitable for discussion before all the world: whoever says so is a sceptic, ignorant of Scripture and incapable of distinguishing between truth and falsehood. Erasmus would sacrifice much to peace; Luther welcomes war. To Luther, Erasmus's prudence and impartiality, even his unwillingness to attack Luther himself, are nothing but scepticism, carelessness, hypocrisy, treachery. Erasmus wishes to serve both God and mammon.

Where Erasmus discusses, Luther affirms: he has no truck with this business of comparing and collating by the light of reason. Erasmus is careful to say he is writing not as a judge but as a commentator: Luther has nothing but contempt and scorn for such an attitude. Can Erasmus not see that once you modify a doctrine to bring it into harmony with reason, faith is destroyed? For Luther, Erasmus is a man without God, lacking all sense of the divine, preaching an ethic without Christ, following the most absurd authorities on the Bible (Jerome and Origen), completely ignorant of what the Scripture really means. His God is the God of philosophers and men of learning, the God of Aristotle; he exalts man above Christ, of whom in his scheme of things man has no need. Luther, on the other hand, prostrates himself before the inscrutable mystery: he affirms the enslavement of the will, the rule of determinism because he *knows*; because the sense of Scripture, so obscure to the searcher by the light of reason, is plainly revealed to the man of faith. Let Erasmus, then, resolve never again to meddle with theology. "God did not grant to you to rise equal to our cause."

To say that Erasmus was hurt would be an understatement. His letter proved how deeply he felt these insults, and in his first letter to Luther in 1526 (in reply to one in which Luther thanked him for his civility!) he asked what advantage could be gained by such invective. He could not find in his conscience that he was an Epicurean or a sceptic or a blasphemer. But by such a temper, intractable to friendship and easily worked upon by harmful influences, Luther had brought ruin on the world.

It was clear that there could be no common ground between two minds so far apart. The curious thing is that they both accuse each other of pride and of excessive use of the intellect in questions that should belong to the heart. To Luther, Erasmus's careful examination of pros and cons speaks of the arrogance of reason. To Erasmus, Luther's self-willed conviction and his determination to define even the undefinable, smacks of overweening self-confidence. Each seemed to himself to have chosen the way of humility, though it was Erasmus, who had not been down to the depths of spiritual despair, who most valued intellectual humility and was content to leave deep problems unsolved.

* * *

Luther's attack did not go unanswered. In Erasmus's two-fold reply, the *Hyperaspistes I* (1526) and *II* (1527) he wrote more vigorously than in the *Essay on*

Free Will, now that he had before him an implacable opponent. And yet the defence of his chosen position was not the only important topic of these two books. It was certainly a vital one, and Luther himself had admitted that Erasmus of all his opponents had gone swiftest to the root of the matter and taken up the essential point. But in *Hyperaspistes I* Erasmus's intention was first to defend himself from all the insults and the innuendos of Luther's violence—to prove that he was neither a sceptic nor a Gallio, and had no axe to grind in the matter and no wordly advantage to attain by way of Rome—and secondly, to develop his own theory that there are only a few dogmas on which the Gospel gives us clear instruction, that the remaining questions may be left unsolved without detriment to our hope of salvation, and that many of them are not suitable to be argued about by all and sundry.

Hyperaspistes II went back to the problem of free will, and recapitulated the lines of thought of the *Essay on Free Will*. More confidently than before, he defined his idea of man's liberty, damaged by the entry of sin into the world, but yet not lost; hanging between two worlds, man has not entire free will nor yet is he totally enslaved, but his will can function truly only when it is co-operating with the grace of God. And Erasmus then launched an attack with all the energy of which he was capable, on Luther's conception of both God and man: Luther's God was dual, on the one hand a crucified God full of love for the world, on the other an inscrutable and terrible Providence whose decrees appear cruel and unjust. Nothing will convince Erasmus that God would ever condemn a soul for what it could not help, and nothing will convince him that the virtues of the pagan philosophers were valueless where they accorded with the Gospel. He points out the many ways in which the rationalism of the ancients was in harmony with Christian thought, and how St. Paul and the Fathers thought of reason (so despised by Luther) as a light reflected from the face of God. Erasmus is at his best as the champion of human liberty against determinism; he would have said with the Lambeth Conference of 1948: "The Gospel is the charter of man's dignity."

Chapter Six

The Middle Way

ERASMUS was nearing sixty at the time of the *De Libero Arbitrio*, and the twelve years he still had to live would bring him to what was then considered as extreme old age. It was not a peaceful or leisurely decline. Up to within a few months of his death he was as busy as ever, keeping Froben's presses moving, writing, revising, editing, re-editing, producing more editions of the New Testament and of the *Adages*, more new Colloquies, more editions of the Fathers—Basil, Ambrose, Chrysostom, Cyprian, Augustine, Jerome, and a host of smaller works, paraphrases of the Psalms, essays on religious subjects like the book on Confession (1524) and on Prayer (1524) or the larger treatise on the art of the preacher (*Ecclesiastes*, 1535), or again discussions on humanistic topics like *The right pronunciation of Latin and Greek* (1528) and the *Ciceronianus*. At the same time there was a continuous output of *Apologiae*, pages quickly written in self-defence, against Stunica, against the theologians of the Sorbonne; and more important than these, the two books in which he replied to Luther's attack in the *De Servo Arbitrio*.

Not only was he never at rest from work, he was also permanently unsettled as to the right place to live. His stay in Bâle lasted eight years, but it was on a temporary basis all the time; we have seen how in

1521 he was being angled for on all sides, and the uncertainty as to which, if any, of these invitations he was finally to accept, went on constantly throughout the following years. Francis I invited him to preside over the new college in Paris for the study of the humanities, but Erasmus was a councillor of the Emperor and could hardly establish himself in the heart of a country at war with the Empire; in the end the Lecteurs Royaux, forerunners of the Collège de France, began their terms of office without Erasmus. Invited more and more pressingly to go to Rome, he confessed that he would prefer to lay his bones there rather than anywhere else, and in the summer of 1522 he actually set out for Italy. It was in the course of this journey that he stayed three weeks with his friend Botzheim, the canon of Constance, in his curiously frescoed house where subjects from the Acts of the Apostles were illustrated side by side with pagan legend; and Erasmus fell in love with the whole place, including the wide peaceful lake and the enclosing mountains with their fringe of forests. Illness overtook him there, and he was forced to return to Bâle. But the idea of seeing Italy again never left him; in the summers of 1523-4-5, he planned the journey and had to relinquish it. Perhaps also an instinct warned him not to endanger his independence; at all events, in the spring of 1527 came the sack of Rome, and there was no room for the leisured visit of a peaceful humanist.

From England the invitations were renewed time after time; Wolsey invited him in 1526, his old friend Mountjoy in 1527, and Erasmus considered the possibility: but when he was preparing to go in 1528, illness supervened, and the news of Henry VIII's intention of obtaining the annulment of his marriage with Catherine of Aragon pointed to difficult times ahead. . . . Vienna, where he was invited twice, did not attract him. . . . The Low Countries provided an obvious refuge and Erasmus considered going there; but there were the vociferous theologians of Louvain, and it was too far from the Froben printing-press, of which he was the mainstay at this time. So, always ready to go and always deciding to stay, Erasmus remained till 1529 at Bâle.

He continued to be the voluminous letter-writer that he had been all his life. The correspondence reveals him to us with all his weaknesses; editors and biographers have always exclaimed at Erasmus's utter disregard for his own reputation. The picture he paints of himself has the sharpest edge; it reveals his touchiness, his sensitivity to opposition, his growing querulousness and anxiety about his failing health, his bad memory for dates and his power of self-deception—but also it preserves for ever his shrewd wit, his sense of fun and his genius for hitting the nail on the head, his indescribable charm and the enthusiastic love he gained and kept from so many friends.

How various they were can be judged from the correspondence, from Erasmus's accounts of his journeys, the reception he got when he stayed overnight in such a town as Freiburg or Besançon. Everywhere he went there were people who were in love with the New Learning and excited at the thought of having Erasmus amongst them, and they were not always the magnates of the town or the ecclesiastical dignitaries.

There is a charming letter[1] describing his journey down the Rhine on his way to Louvain in September 1518, when they stopped at Boppard, the customs frontier between the Emperor and the Archbishop of Trèves; while the customs examination was going on, Erasmus went for a walk on the bank, and someone recognised him and said to the customs officer: "There he is!" The customs officer was a certain Christopher Eschenfelder, and he had a passion for the New Learning. Full of joy, he took Erasmus into his house, where some of Erasmus's books were lying on the table among the official papers, called his wife and children and all his friends, and sent out wine to the sailors to keep the boat waiting a little longer. Erasmus wrote a merry letter to him on reaching Louvain:[2]

"What a delightful surprise, to find such a friend at Boppard! A customs-officer who cares for the Muses and good learning! Christ reproached the Pharisees, saying that the publicans and harlots should go before them into the kingdom of heaven. What a disgrace it is to priests and monks! they live in ease and luxury, while officials spend their time in study; all *their* thoughts are of what they shall eat and what they shall drink, while Eschenfelder divides his time between his Imperial Majesty and his books. It was easy to see what an idea you had formed of me beforehand; I am lucky if the sight of me has not spoiled your dream. That red wine of yours found favour with the captain's wife, a great bouncing woman with a fine thirst. She gulped it

[1] Allen, III, p. 867.
[2] Happily translated by P. S. Allen in *Erasmus*, p. 14.

down, and would give no one else a chance. This made her quarrelsome, and she nearly slew her servant-girl with a big spoon; then going up on deck, she attacked her husband and nearly toppled him into the Rhine. That's what comes of your wine!"

Or as another example, there is the letter written in 1525 by Erasmus Schets, a merchant and banker of Antwerp, who had admired Erasmus from afar and seized the opportunity afforded by a parcel of letters which had to be forwarded on to him from Spain. Schets slipped in one of his own, describing himself as another Erasmus who has sometimes had the good luck to be mistaken for the great one, "You who stand alone in all the world and are incomparable, you who through your most learned and truly religious Paraphrases have brought heavenly doctrine and the words of the Gospel within the reach of human frailty, so that anyone who wishes may read and understand and come out of darkness into light. . . ."

The letter goes on into a description of the enthusiasm for Erasmus's works which is felt in Spain, and how everyone hopes that before he dies he will write a Paraphrase of the Psalms. And finally, how is Erasmus's health, and what enchantment can possibly be keeping him at Bâle and away from his friends in Brabant? Is it true that he fears the lack of Burgundy wine, which he cannot do without? "Don't be afraid of that; if that is all that stands in the way, you need not fear to return. We will see to providing you not only with Burgundy, but with Persian and Indian wine if there were any need for that." It was strange that the man in Europe who had the greatest number of such friends should be so conscious of being a "dweller in tents," living in uncertainty and never till his dying day feeling that he had a settled home.

Strange, but highly significant of his relationship to the Europe of his day. No one had touched more hearts and minds, his books were everywhere and his name a household word, but it was becoming clearer every day that there was no place for him in the battle-field where the opposing parties were lining up in preparation for a savage struggle. To go to any place where he might appear to ally himself with either party was to abandon the position he had chosen. It is to Erasmus's eternal credit that he never flew to the protection of Rome, which would have silenced once and for all his most vociferous enemies. The tale of his controversies with the opponents of reform, during the years he spent at Bâle, is astonishing : one wonders how he found time to attend to the continuous output of learned work which was unceasingly flowing from his pen. After the conflict with Stunica in Spain, there was the campaign of Béda of the Sorbonne. This man, Noel Bédier, had become syndic of the Faculty of Theology (an office he seems to have proposed himself) and had been the successor of Standonck as Principal of the Collège de Montaigu, of which Erasmus had such dark memories. From 1525 Béda led with great determination a violent campaign against the evangelical leaders of reform, especially Erasmus and Lefèvre d'Etaples. It was Béda who urged on the Faculty to an examination and censure of Erasmus's works, first the Paraphrase on St. Luke and the Exposition of the Lord's Prayer, then several small works translated by Louis de Berquin, a fervent admirer of Erasmus, including the *Complaint of Peace;* these condemnations were issued in 1524 and 1525. In 1526 it was the turn of the *Colloquies.* Béda himself published in the same year, with the approval of the Faculty, three volumes of *Annotations* enumerating the errors of Lefèvre and Erasmus, censuring passages culled from the notes on the New Testament, the *Paraphrases,* the *Enchiridion,* and several smaller works such as the *De Esu Carnium,* on fasting. Erasmus carried on a long correspondence with Béda, and in 1527 published a long and minute defence, treating Béda however with the utmost contempt.

Simultaneously the theologians returned to the attack in Spain, where the appearance of a Spanish translation of the *Enchiridion* launched a new offensive. In the Low Countries the old opposition was still going on, led by the monks of Louvain; Erasmus's New Testament was publicly burnt at Bois-le-Duc. Even in Italy the leaders of criticism against him were not silent; he took up his pen in 1529 to write the *Apology to Alberto Pio,* prince of Carpi, who was voicing a more moderate but no less sinister hostility, backed by the monasteries of Rome and the legate Aleander. This defence followed close on the heels of the *Apology against the monks of Spain* (1528). Everywhere Erasmus recognised his enemies in the monastic orders.

The attacks from the Sorbonne were the most deadly of all these efforts to drown or silence the voice of Erasmus. Paris being the home and headquarters of the supporters of the scholastic theology, it was natural that the theologians of the Sorbonne should see in him an enemy insidiously powerful and more dangerous even than Luther. The case of Berquin was a potent warning of how far they would go. Berquin, who translated some of Erasmus's shorter writings and wrote to him the letters of a disciple, was one of those well-meaning, reckless enthusiasts who can do so much to ruin a cause. Erasmus treated his letters with courtesy and reserve; he sensed Berquin's hot imprudence and he suspected the translations of being doctored. And so they were; Berquin being one of those false friends who in their enthusiasm tried to push Erasmus willy-nilly into the camp of Luther. Berquin had inserted in his versions of Erasmus extracts from Luther and the even more revolutionary Farel. Nothing loth to expend on the rash Frenchman the anger they felt against an Erasmus well out of reach, the Sorbonne arrested him twice and saw him slip out of their clutches through the favour of the King. Emboldened by his apparent immunity, Berquin carried the war into the enemy's camp by arraigning Béda himself (1529). But the theologians were not to be trifled with; they prevailed on the Parlement to arrest Berquin for possessing prohibited books, to try him and sentence him to perpetual imprisonment. Berquin appealed to the King and the Pope, but his enemies had the upper hand; they altered the decree to sentence of death, and Berquin was summarily taken to the Place de Grève, and there hanged and burnt, before Francis I could once more intervene.

To such lengths Erasmus's enemies would carry their fear and detestation of his principle of reasoned enquiry into the Scriptures. On the other side the picture was no less sombre. Luther did not reply to the *Hyperaspistes*: there was little use in replying, since the gulf that separated his stark theology from Erasmus's Christian humanism was so clear. Erasmus kept in contact with Luther's wise and moderate friend Melancthon, but he watched the course of the other reformers with sadness and distaste. They were already in conflict with each other; the Swiss reformers, Zwingli in particular, were by far to outstrip Luther in their radical views. "When I admonished Zwingli in a friendly way he wrote back disdainfully: 'What you know is of no use to us; what we know is not for you.' As if he had been caught up like Paul to the third heaven and learnt some mystery which was hidden to us earthly creatures!" In 1524 Erasmus had had several contacts with Guillaume Farel, one of the most violent of the Swiss reformers, and after a stormy interview had had him expelled from the city by the council of Bâle (like Hutten in 1523), thus making him into an even more implacable enemy. But Bâle itself was falling more and more under the influence of the reforming party, led by Œcolampadius, who knew Erasmus from of old (had he not read the proofs of the New Testament in Froben's printing-house?) but was now turning firmly against him. He had finally accepted the radical reforms of Zwingli, and was carrying with him a majority of the people of Bâle. Every moderate publication of Erasmus's, such as his book on confession, irritated them more.

He was treated with deference by the authorities, and in 1525 the Council asked him for his advice on the religious question; he sent a fairly long reply, suggesting three lines of conciliation. In the first place, supervision of the Press so that nothing is published, either Lutheran or Catholic, which is not in terms of civil discussion; suppress anonymous and libellous publications. Secondly, on the points at issue—ceremonies, images, the Mass, fasting, confession—let there be complete toleration until it is possible to have the matter thrashed out by a really competent Council of the Church, including of course the leaders of the reformed churches. Finally, supervise the transformation of the monastic orders and the priesthood which is going on; obtain official sanction for the abandonment by some of their vows, and official permission for certain priests to marry; avoid a stampede. Erasmus said nothing of the great burning questions of the day. His opinions were well known, and he realised the uselessness of airing them again in this instance, before men who judged even Luther timid. Such hearers could not possibly have been shaken by the reiteration of the precepts of the *Philosophia Christi*.

He watched from day to day the progress of the Reformation. The restriction or suppression of the monasteries, if done with circumspection and without causing distress, seems to him a useful measure, if only it had the approval of the constituted authorities. Some things however he cannot approve, especially the views of the Swiss reformers on the Eucharist; where Luther admitted two sacraments only, Baptism and Holy Communion, Zwingli and his followers had acquired the name of Sacramentarians by denying to the sacrifice of the Eucharist the name or nature of a sacrament. "Most people here hate the Mass," wrote Erasmus, "and some teach publicly that there is nothing in the Eucharist but bread and wine."

The Council attempted to keep the balance between the parties, but Œcolampadius was too strong for them. January 1528 saw the city on the brink of civil war; the Council discouraged the Catholic party from offering resistance. On February 8th, a public rising demanded the dismissal of those members of the Council favourable to Rome. Next day there was a general attack on the churches, the crowd surging in to smash the images and break the stained glass. Erasmus described it graphically in a letter to his friend Pirckheimer; he must have watched sadly from the windows of his house as the mob wreaked its will on the inanimate objects of a too-superstitious cult. Perhaps his mind went back to the *Enchiridion*, to his own efforts to demonstrate that it would be better to follow the Sermon on the Mount than treasure a relic, however authentic, of Christ's physical presence. This kind of clean sweep was not at all what he had intended to recommend. "The Council has kept the riot in check by allowing the smiths and carpenters to take whatever they liked out of the churches. . . . Not a statue has been left, in the churches, in the porches, on the façades or in the monasteries; all the frescoes have been whitewashed over. Everything which would burn has been set on fire, everything else hacked into little pieces. Neither value nor artistry prevailed to save anything." Monks and nuns are to leave the town or abandon their habit, the Mass has been suppressed, the service now consists of a sermon and Psalms sung in German, the Communion is purely a symbol. The Lutherans hold some churches, but the Sacramentarians are in the majority, and there are Anabaptists who are hated by the other parties and have no churches of their own; Erasmus seems to regard these with some sympathy. Altogether the prospect is a dismal one, and Erasmus, conscious of the hatred of the Sacramentarians, feels that if he stays much longer he will meet the fate of the images, and that his presence in the transformed town, where he fears that "the reign of the Pharisees will be followed by that of the pagans" can be construed as a tacit consent. He now seriously made up his mind to go.

But where? Of all the refuges that were open to him, he chose Freiburg in Breisgau, an Austrian town and strongly Catholic (on the superstitious side, he said, but perhaps that was better than the tyranny of the new churches). In the University there he had friends and admirers, and it was not too far from Bâle for him to keep in touch with the heirs of Froben—the great printer himself was dead. Freiburg then it was to be, but to Erasmus, Freiburg represented only the first stage of a long journey; his restless mind saw prospects of travelling on. Actually he was to live there six years, and only to return to Bâle to die. The Council of Bâle and Œcolampadius made some formal attempts to retain him, but his mind was made up; he sent his furniture and belongings off in a couple of waggons and on April 13th left Bâle himself by boat. The plan was to go down the Rhine from Bâle as far as Neuenberg, and then on to Freiburg on horseback, and he was accompanied by his devoted friend Boniface Amerbach, the young Bâle printer. Given the state of the city, it seemed to Erasmus's friends that it would be preferable for him to leave quietly from a point on the river that was not too public, but the Council would not allow this—why, he could not quite understand; probably they wished to avoid giving the impression that their most notable resident was being hounded into exile. So Erasmus embarked from the usual place near the great stone bridge, under the soaring towers of the reformed Cathedral, at noon on April 13th; and no word was spoken against him.

* * *

The first weeks at Freiburg were a relief. "I like this well-behaved town," he wrote, "I haven't heard anyone speak ill of anyone else!" The Council had offered him a spacious house, constructed for the Archduke Maximilian but never finished. Into this he moved with his furniture, his presentation plate (at this time admirers were frequently sending him gold and silver cups, some of which may be seen in the museum at Bâle), his servant-pupils and his crabbed housekeeper Margaret, whose bad temper exercised his patience, he said, as Socrates was disciplined by Xantippe. The journey seemed to have done him good rather than harm, and the first letters from Freiburg are remarkably cheerful. Among other pleasant things was an amicable literary friendship with another refugee from Bâle, Ambrose Storch. Erasmus was up in arms at once when hostile criticism came his way, but when his findings were disputed in a friendly spirit he eagerly welcomed discussion. It was with a sense of relief that he turned to a field of argument where he could feel more at home (his own notes on the New Testament). But the outside world remained chaotic, and one piece of news perturbed him greatly: the very day on which he left Bâle had seen the end of Louis de Berquin, and Erasmus sorrowfully tells the tale in a long letter to a friend. He confesses that from reading all Berquin's letters he had

had the most sinister impression of coming disaster, even when the unfortunate man was congratulating himself. It is no joke to make an enemy like the Sorbonne: "a Faculty never dies." The whole story has moved Erasmus deeply. "The idea of burning a man because he is wrong! I wonder where they got it from." The raging followers of Béda will be encouraged to further violence. Yet Erasmus brings himself to say that perhaps it is better to err in the direction of superstition like the French, than to overturn all order and damn the Church as the work of the devil, as they do in Germany. Which is one to choose? He is sorry about Berquin. However, if he died with a good conscience, as seems likely by his serene bearing, he is happy. "To be condemned, quartered, hanged, burnt, beheaded, may be the lot of good men as of evil. He alone is happy who is acquitted when God is his judge."

The first thing Erasmus did in Freiburg was to write a preface for the Froben edition of St. Augustine, which he had been labouring on for five years. It came out at last, ten large volumes, an undertaking which had at times seemed too large for his failing strength. All through 1530 his health was wretched and he did little beyond writing prefaces for the books being issued by the Frobens, but in 1531 he was encouraging them to prepare an edition of Basil in Greek—the first edition; and he seems to have directed this enterprise from Freiburg. His next task was to finish a book on the art of preaching, *Ecclesiastes*, which he had had in hand for twelve years. It came out in 1535. Simultaneously he was working on several shorter things, especially Paraphrases of the Psalms; one of them was his very last work, and he dedicated it to Christopher Eschenfelder, the enthusiastic customs-officer who had welcomed him so warmly long ago.

One of these Psalms, *How amiable are Thy dwellings*, gave him an opportunity to voice again his own point of view, so when the little work was published in 1533 it had the title *On restoring concord in the Church*. It shows Erasmus nearly at the end of his life, looking at the scene before him, at the violent defenders of the old system with their fanatical persecution, the countless reformed churches at variance with each other and instituting new practices and new tyrannies. To this chaos spoke the old voice of a much-loved and much-hated man. This time he did not avoid the definite subjects of contention. He went through them all: Freewill, prayers for the dead, invocation of the saints, images, relics, confession, the Mass, holy-days, fasting. How are people to agree on these much-debated topics? Erasmus's simple answer is: Tolerate each other.

There are two essentials, he says, which we must seek if we are to ask God to bring back peace to our midst. One is simply a matter of morality, not of theology; if we all did our job, not only Pope, Princes, magistrates and priests, but merchants, millers, smiths and tailors, we should be nearer concord. Let no one say "It's the fashion," or "That is not done," but let us bend our energies to live well. The other essential is to remember that it is not safe or useful to depart lightly from all that has been handed down by tradition. Going through the specific subjects of difference he says of each one: abandon superstition, set no store by little things, obey your own judgment

216

but let others obey theirs. In the matter of prayers to the saints, for instance. Some individuals have been in their lifetime so ennobled by God that at their prayer He drove out evil spirits and raised the dead. It seems to some people a true and religious idea that those saintly characters should not be without power before God now. And those who hold a different opinion, and invoke with a sincere heart Father, Son, and Holy Ghost, should tolerate those who equally sincerely appeal to the Saints. Certainly let us get rid of the superstitions attached to the practice. Yet a simple and devout heart must be tolerated, even if it holds a little error; "Christ loves simple souls, and will hear us even if the saints do not, and will grant our prayers if not through them at least for their sake."

It is the same with images and relics. First of all let us guard against idolatry. But we can do this without smashing up the statues and tearing down the paintings, which are a kind of silent poetry. Far from removing all pictures, Erasmus thinks every house would be better if it were fit to have the life of Christ depicted on its walls; probably he was remembering his dream in the *Religious Banquet*, or Botzheim's house at Constance. So too with relics; we can tolerate those who cherish vestiges of saintly persons, although we know that the important thing is to imitate their lives. Above all, let us follow our own choice, allow others to do the same, and avoid unnecessary insistence on trifles. As to Confession, Erasmus himself did not believe it was instituted by Christ, though he does not say so here. What he says is that it would be as well to preserve it, as an old and useful custom, and use it rightly—not rushing to the priest as soon as anything has gone wrong, or otherwise treating it mechanically, but confessing our sins to God, and making confession at a suitable opportunity. Similarly let us get rid of the customs which encumber the institution of the Mass, especially the custom of private masses; but there is no need to discard the basic constituents of the service itself, accepted for so many centuries. In all things the word is: choose your own way, tolerate others, until a general ruling on the subject has been made.

Was Erasmus going back on the boldness of his earlier days when he spoke this pacific message?

The Lutherans of his own day were ready enough to accuse him of looking back after putting his hand to the plough. To insist on tolerance, even of those things which he had formerly seen as so dangerous, seemed to be throwing away the results of his struggle for a spiritual religion. There was the fear and weariness of an old man in the ending of the essay, where he threatened the iconoclasts and promoters of civil war with the wrath of the Kings of Europe. But he still spoke as one who would tolerate the old practices for the sake of peace, but who did not himself believe in them. He was still refusing to take sides. And the fury this attitude caused in all his opponents produced the accusation of cowardice which still clings to his name; one of his best modern biographers writes of the "tragic defect running through his whole personality, this refusal or inability ever to draw ultimate conclusions."[1]

This judgment seems to ignore the fact that to Erasmus the middle way which he proposed was an

[1] Huizinga, *Erasmus*, p. 187.

ultimate conclusion. He might advise the world to wait for the ruling of a Council of the Church, but the tolerance he advocated was no temporary measure; he had said often enough that there were truths beyond the grasp of man's intellect, and that it was useless to insist on definitions. He believed in the real presence of Christ in Holy Communion, but he had always blamed the efforts of theological schools to define the manner of that presence, and the doctrine of transubstantiation appeared to him as an unnecessary adjunct to the early beliefs of the Church. Luther's mania for defining and explaining was as bad as the complex theories of a Duns Scotus. To Erasmus an ounce of brotherly charity was worth a pound of metaphysical speculation. He believed that a great deal could be discovered as to the Christian way of life from a correct and courageous searching of the Scriptures, but he also believed that when face to face with the unknowable, what the Christian had to do was to take off his shoes like Moses before the burning bush and say: "This is holy ground." It was certainly not his duty to crush and wipe out other Christians who approached those mysteries from another angle. "The modernism of Erasmus, far from all confessional strictness, reduces dogma to the purest essence of spiritual evangelism, and wishes the Catholic Church to open its doors freely to all men of good will without exacting from men's minds a conformity which Jesus did not impose on them."[1]

He had been preaching this doctrine ever since 1501. The *Enchiridion* had raised all these questions as to ceremonies, images, relics, and so forth, and had

[1] Renaudet, ap. cit., p. 181.

made an impassioned plea for a sense of proportion, for the recognition of the fact that only spiritual values counted in the life of a Christian. But it had not argued for the complete abolition of all these symbols, only for their relegation to their proper place, as toys for those who were yet children in Christ, but who must be taught to look beyond them to the true knowledge of what religion means. And to Erasmus it means quite simply the attempt to imitate the character of Jesus. This attempt can only be founded on knowledge; and the interpretation of the documents which preserve for us the sayings and acts of Jesus appeared to Erasmus the most important activity, englobing in itself all the findings of modern and antique science. To free the mind for the task of explaining and understanding the Gospel is his aim. Thus the exercise of the powers of reason, without trammels and without prejudice, is placed at the service of a very humble ideal of Christian life, such as Erasmus had seen developed by the teachers of his youth.

The notes on the New Testament and the *Paraphrases* had continued this work of liberation, and in 1522–4, in several smaller writings (*De Esu Carnium, Modus Orandi Deum*) Erasmus had shown how he conceived of a Church in which it would be possible to think of spiritual values first. He does not recommend the immediate abolition of all abuses, but sees them as gradually vanishing before the advance of enlightenment. Let observances and ceremonies be considered as non-essential; they will soon lose their tyrannical hold over men's consciences. Let the Church seriously consider the question of the marriage of the clergy, lighten the burden of abstinence, abrogate the multitude of rules and regulations. Preserve the Latin liturgy, let the unlearned have a translation, but let all general prayers, hymns and teaching be in the vulgar tongue. Let the Church of its own will discard everything that leads to hypocrisy, formalism, sterility of mind or feeling. One is reminded that a little later Erasmus was to say plainly to Luther: this Church that we have is far from perfect, but I shall stay in it until I find a better.

In these circumstances, it seems clear that Erasmus would have betrayed all that he ever stood for, if he had allied himself with either side. To denounce Luther would have been to reinforce the ranks of the monks who supported that formalism which he so hated. To join the reformers would have been to throw his weight against that reform within the Church which was his hope, but also it would have meant assenting to an intolerance and a formalism of a different kind. Erasmus's ideal church was neither the one nor the other.

As regards the assertion made by M. Huizinga that his final position is a withdrawal, two things are to be said. The first is that the views on relics and observances expressed in the essay *On restoring concord in the Church* are the same as those expressed in the *Enchiridion*, but the emphasis is different. In 1501 Erasmus had advocated tolerance, but he had been more impressed by the need for spiritual regeneration. In 1533 he still says that the virtues of the saints are to be treasured rather than their old shoes, but he has seen the image-breakers at work in Bâle, and he is inclined to emphasise the need for toleration. Secondly, one new theory did add itself to Erasmus's opinions in course of time, and that was due to his reading of the Fathers; it was the belief in a progressive revelation to the Church, and it made him the more cautious in his treatment of tradition.

*　　*　　*

Apart from these reservations, it seems that Erasmus's mistake, if mistake there was, lay not in vacillation but in over-consistency, in the fact that he did not adapt himself to the changing scene. Since his brush with Luther he had withdrawn himself from active intervention, and had become more of a spectator than ever. But all his contemplation of the warring currents of the sixteenth century did not convince him that his middle way was acceptable to nobody, and that the time for toleration was not yet. He went on preaching to the deaf, and though he had a wide influence he made no party; as he had said, he created no Erasmists. Perhaps the reformed churches of Europe are nearer in the twentieth century than they have ever been before to his ideal of harmony in diversity. But in his own lifetime he saw failure, and his last days were saddened by increasing signs of the bitter religious wars ahead. He had meant to dedicate the *Ecclesiastes* to John Fisher, bishop of Rochester, one of his oldest friends. But by the time it was ready and he had returned to Bâle to see it through the press, Fisher had lost his life on the scaffold and it was the turn of Thomas More to lay his down too. It was 1535, and Erasmus was ready to follow them. Nearly all his old friends were dead, and in his solitude he doubted the sincerity of those who were left. A gleam of consolation must have come to him from the kindly messages of the new Pope, Paul III, but to the offers of advancement and the suggestion of a cardinal's hat Erasmus replied that he could accept nothing. He wanted to die as he had lived. And so for a few months, almost bed-ridden in Jerome Froben's friendly white house in Bâle, he worked at the new task, an edition of Origen, to add to the monumental series of the Fathers. He was not destined to finish it. On July 12th, 1536 the end came to a long life. Luther said Erasmus died without God and without hope, *sine lux, sine crux, sine Deus*. But the friends who were with him knew differently. It has always seemed strange and pathetic that the last words of so great a Latinist should be in the tongue of his childhood, and that "Jesu, misericordia!" should change with his last breath to "Lieve God."

* * *

If Erasmus's middle way was doomed to failure, as far as the confessional struggles of his own century were concerned, it would be untrue to suggest that it had no effect on his own generation, and no meaning for later times. That mellow, balanced sanity has always cast its spell, representing as it does the perfect work of the classical spirit tempered by the Christian ideal. It is indeed the middle way, not only between Catholic and Protestant, but between the mind and the heart. It needs on the one hand a liberated intellect, on the other a realisation of the realms outside the reach of reason; a serene faith and a warm love of mankind are essentials to it. It is the climate of the mind in which humour grows, friendship blossoms and

223

tolerance cultivates the flowers of the spirit: a tolerance resulting not from indolence but from decision and clear thinking. There have always been individuals, and groups of individuals, who saw the Erasmian spirit as leading the way to a Promised Land of mental peace.

But this is an influence which can hardly be estimated. How far can his ideas be said to have had a definite repercussion on his own century and succeeding ones, and what was the net result of his influence? The answer is at least fourfold. His character in part eludes us yet, but the results of his work have often been assessed, and there is no doubt about their importance in at least four domains of thought.

The most obvious results of his influence are in the spread of classical culture in Europe, not only through the tools which he put into people's hands, the texts, the Adages, but also because of his sensitivity to the qualities of the classical style, his interest in the use of language as a clear medium of thought, as the expression of everything human. "He accustomed a whole world to another and more fluent mode of expression."[1] He did a great deal by his own personal labours to put the antique world within reach of his contemporaries, and he set others going, by the example of what could be done, by his unfailing encouragement —his letters show how he was the central figure in a network of scholarship—by his continuous interest in education and in the young. He was the only one of the Humanists who wished to extend the knowledge of the classics to all the world; he wrote for a wide public, not an exclusive one. It would be hard to over-

[1] Huizinga, op. cit., p. 243.

estimate his importance as a disseminator of the new ideas. If one were to regard the Renaissance simply as the impact of classical literature on the modern world one might be tempted to say that for a time Erasmus *was* the Renaissance. More than any other single person he made that impact possible.

From the point of view of religious thought, it has been seen that his ideas were not fulfilled. But this is not to say that his influence in this sphere was not considerable. Few of his contemporaries remained in the tolerant atmosphere of the Philosophy of Christ, but most of them passed through it, at least of those who were in any way touched with the spirit of reform. On both sides of the conflict he had his kindred spirits, who strove for reconciliation until it seemed finally impossible. In his lifetime both sides cast him off, but ever since both have claimed him for their own—an unfailing sign of the perfect balance which he achieved. And his work on the New Testament had a double result; by encouraging the current interest in the Bible it had incalculable effects in his own time, and by opening the field of exegetical research it began a process which was to lead to a new attitude of mind, a process which is not yet complete in our own day. "The question which Erasmus raised was: 'What is the Bible?' Neither he nor his opponents saw where he was tending; if he could have foreseen, he would have been shocked, no doubt, but not deterred. For God to him was *via, vita, veritas*; and Truth shirks no questions, however startling."[1]

This leads us to the third and most controversial part of Erasmus's spiritual heritage—his contribution

[1] Allen, *Erasmus* .p. 73.

to the rise of rationalism in Europe. As we have seen, Erasmus could hardly be called a rationalist himself; in his mind intellectual truth and spiritual truth were distinct, but they were not divorced, and the one was to supplement the other. But it was easy for that simple faith, so much less transmissible, to be left on one side while the confidence in reason which Erasmus shared with all other humanists went its triumphant way. It is not for us to trace the pedigree of rationalism through the successors of Erasmus such as Montaigne, to Descartes and the English seventeenth-century philosophers, and beyond them to the eighteenth century, heralded by Bayle who when he was writing his *Nouvelles de la République des Lettres*, had the bright idea of decorating his title-page with the figure of Erasmus from the statue at Rotterdam. For the rationalist and anticlerical writers of the eighteenth century Erasmus was (by implication if not by statement) the person his Lutheran and Catholic opponents had accused him of being, the sceptic, the modern Lucian, the unbeliever, the hidden atheist, who undermined authority by his wit, did the Church deadly blows by his satire and set reason above all other functions of the mind. They were repeating the old reproaches, but to them it was a matter for congratulation and Erasmus appeared to them truly enlightened. It continually happens that one facet of a writer's work catches the light of posterity, and a lack of balance in the popular notion of his significance results. For a time this was the case with Erasmus, but it has long been rectified, and the Christian character of his humanism is clear to us today. Yet he stands before us still as the apostle of common sense, and a great liberator of the mind.

Finally, there is the side of Erasmus's thought which seems now more modern than any; his tolerance, his pacifism, his vision of international relations, his suggestions—tentative as they were—for arbitration and the suppression of war. Religious tolerance on the lines he suggested we have long enjoyed, and we are perhaps drawing still nearer to a fuller understanding of it. International understanding is nearer to us than it was to him, but still a vision of the future. Here his personal fastidiousness and his love for the things of peace led him to be unusually prophetic; and his own position, virtually stateless, equally in contact with all the countries which constituted his Europe, makes him seem curiously in touch with the situation brought about in our own day by rapid communications and a shrinking world. We know that in many of his proposals he was looking backwards rather than forwards, but his love of peace burns as brightly for us as for his contemporaries, his writings on peace are as directly relevant to our situation as to theirs and it is not without value to us that he should have hoped so passionately for a Christian understanding between nations. If ever the United States of Europe are born out of the birth-pangs of many wars, it will be a victory not foreign to the spirit of Erasmus.

Short Bibliography

(Literature on Erasmus and his times is very extensive; the following are some of the key books on the subject)

(a) WRITINGS OF ERASMUS

The standard edition is *Erasmi Opera*, Leyden, 1703.

Opus Epistolarum Des. Erasmi Roterodami, denuo recognitum et auctum, ed. P. S. and H. M. Allen, Oxford, 1906–47.

Epistles of Erasmus from his earliest Letters to his fifty-first year. English translation by F. M. Nichols, London, 1901–17.

The Handsome Weapon of a Christian Knight (translation of the *Enchiridion Militis Christiani*) published by Wynkyn de Worde, 1534.

The Praise of Folly, ed. H. M. Allen, Oxford, 1913.

The Complaint of Peace, tr. T. Paynell, 1559, reprinted by M. J. Hutten, New York, 1946.

The Education of a Christian Prince, ed. L. K. Born, Columbia University Press, 1936.

Essai sur le Libre Arbitre, tr. P. Mesnard, Paris, 1945.

The Whole Familiar Colloquies of Erasmus of Rotterdam, tr. N. Bailey, London, 1887.

(b) BIOGRAPHY, ETC.

ALLEN, P. S.: *The Age of Erasmus*. Oxford, 1914.

ALLEN, P. S.: *Erasmus: lectures and wayfaring sketches*, Oxford, 1934.

BATAILLON, M.: *Erasme et l'Espagne*, Paris, 1937.

CHAMBERS, R. W.: *Thomas More*, London, 1935.

FROUDE, J. A.: *The Life and Letters of Erasmus*, London, 1894.

HUIZINGA, J.: *Erasmus*, tr. F. Hopman, London, 1924.

MESNARD, P.: *L'Essor de la philosophie politique au seizième siècle*, Paris, 1936.

RENAUDET, A.: *Erasme, sa pensée religieuse*, Paris, 1926.

RENAUDET, A.: *Etudes Erasmiennes*, Paris, 1939.

SMITH (Preserved): *Erasmus; a study of his life, ideals and place in history*, New York and London, 1923.

Index

229

INDEX

St. Christopher, iii
Ste. Geneviève, Abbey of, 23
Ste. Geneviève, Shrine of, 28
St. James of Compostella, 111
St. Lebwin's School, 7
St. Mary's College, 42
St. Omer, 46 note
St. Paul's (Dean of), 41
St. Peter's (Rome), 158
St. Stephen's (Westminster), 88
St. Thomas of Canterbury, 67, 112
Sallust, 19
Sardou, Victorien, 103
Saxony (Elector of), 168
Scaliger, 58
Schets, Erasmus, 206
Schoolmen, The, 155, 160–4, 182
Scotists, The, 65
Scotland, 60
Scott, Sir Walter, 103
Scrivener (Dr.), 75, 76 note
Seneca, xix, 32, 72, 130, 132
Servatius, 17–18
Severnbergen, Peter of, 5
Shakespeare, William, 103
's Hertogenbosch, 14
Ship of Fools, The, 92
Siena, 59
Sintheim, John, 12
Sion, 16
Sixtin, John, 42
Smith, Preserved, 33 note, 102 note, 110
Socrates, 33, 80
Sorbonne, The, 24, 43, 70, 189, 202, 207–8
Spain, 206–8
Spalatin, 167
Standonck, John, 23, 207
Statius, 19
Staupitz, John, 162
Steyn, Convent of, 4, 16–18, 28, 61, 88
Stoics, 80

Storch, Ambrose, 214
Stuart, Alexander, 58, 60
Stunica (Zúñiga), 183, 189, 202, 207
Suetonius, 32
Sylva Odarum, 26

Teaching of Children, The, xix
Terence, 12, 16, 19, 21, 32
Testament, New, 73–85, 220
Tetzel, John, 158
Thomas à Kempis, 8, 12, 18, 21
Thomists, 65
Tibullus, 19
Titian, 58
Tournehem, 45
Trèves (Archbishop of), 205
Turin, University of, 55

Utopia, 124, 137
Utrecht, 20

Valla, Lorenzo, xix, 19, 44, 75
Vatican, The, 174, 177, 186
Veere (Lady of), 45
Vendôme, 119
Venice 25, 57–9, 115, 126
Vienna, 204
Virgil, 12, 19–21
Voltaire, 3, 90, 123–4, 127, 137, 139

Walsingham, Our Lady of, 112
Warham, William, 54, 65, 71
Wartburg, The, xx, 167
Watson, John, xx, 89–90
Werner, Nicholas, 28
Westminster, 88
Winckel, Peter, 6, 14–15
Windesheim, Abbey of, 8, 23

235